외국어 전문 출판 브랜드

맛있는 books

South Korea Map

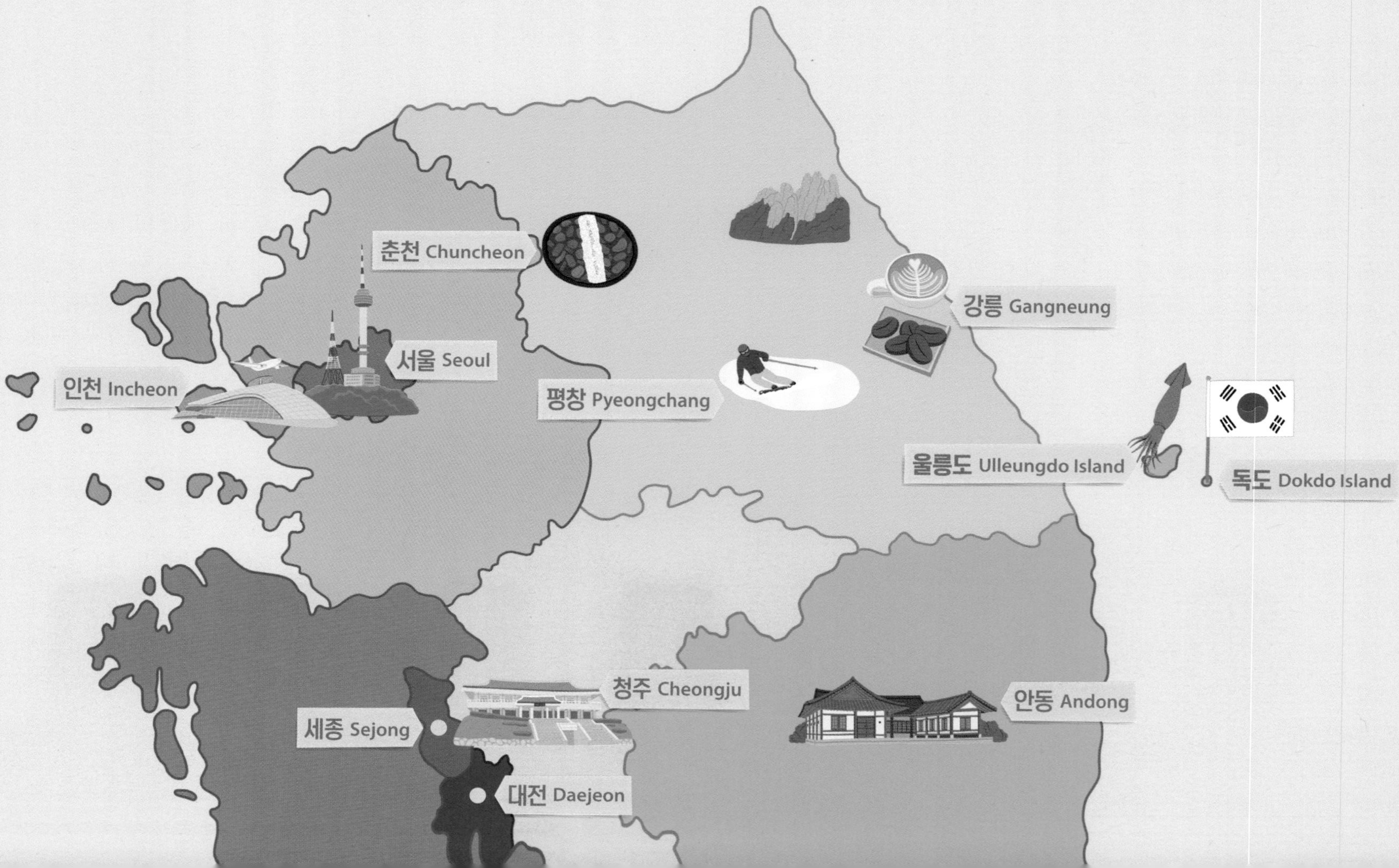

독도 Dokdo Island

강릉 Gangneung

울릉도 Ulleungdo Island

안동 Andong

청주 Cheongju

평창 Pyeongchang

춘천 Chuncheon

서울 Seoul

대전 Daejeon

세종 Sejong

인천 Incheon

경주 Gyeongju

울산 Ulsan

부산 Busan

대구 Daegu

여수 Yeosu

전주 Jeonju

담양 Damyang

광주 Gwangju

제주도 Jejudo Island

경기도 Gyeonggi-do
강원도 Gangwon-do
충청북도 Chungcheongbuk-do
충청남도 Chungcheongnam-do
전라북도 Jeollabuk-do
전라남도 Jeollanam-do
경상북도 Gyeongsangbuk-do
경상남도 Gyeongsangnam-do

Let's Speak Korean
for Beginners

맛있는
한국어
첫걸음

Kim Misook

맛있는 books

Let's Speak
Korean
for Beginners

First Published	July 15, 2022
Second Printing	December 10, 2024

Author	Kim, Misook
Translator	Lee, Wonseog
Proofreaders	Korean Society of Translators, Evely Ong Yih Yuan, Romika Chandra, Ko Wanting
Planning	JRC language research institute
Publisher	Kim, Hyojung

ISBN	979-11-6148-064-0 13710
Price	19,500 won

맛있는 books
www.booksJRC.com

7F JRC Bldg., 54 Myeongdal-ro, Seocho-gu, Seoul, 06708 Republic of Korea
Tel: Marketing Dept. 02-567-3861 / 02-567-3837   Editorial Dept. 02-567-3860   Fax: 02-567-2471

천 리 길도 한 걸음부터

A journey of a thousand miles must begin with the first step

Interest in the Korean language continues to grow steadily. Recently, more and more people are studying Korean alone, so I, as a Korean teacher, am just happy and grateful for their interest and love.

『Let's Speak Korean for Beginners 맛있는 한국어 첫걸음』 was composed with the desire to let them study Korean in a more fun and effective as the title suggests.

I have presented the beginner-level expression, which you must know when learning alone, and cultural and grammatical tips that are helpful to the learning.

It also introduces places to visit and food in Korea so that you can study with fun and interest as if you were traveling in Korea.

It is not easy to learn a foreign language alone, but if you study it step by step, you will find that your Korean is improving.

I would like to express my gratitude to 맛있는books for meticulously proceeding with the publication of this book.

There is a Korean proverb that says, "천 리 길도 한 걸음부터(A journey of a thousand miles must begin with the first step.)" This means it is important to start properly when going a long way, meaning that the beginning is very significant.

Finally, we all here hope that this book helps you in the first step of learning Korean with fun and interest.

Kim Misook

• How to Use This book •

• For this week

You can check the travel destinations and learning contents each week through maps and vivid illustrations at a glance.

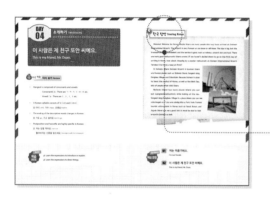

You can review the past lessons and check the learning points and the key sentences in advance.

You can see the theme travel destination with the picture in advance.

• 맛있는 핵심 문법 Grammar

Learn the core grammar and expressions, and check the tips together.

• 실력 다지기 Practice

You can make sure that the core grammar is yours with various exercises.

• 맛있는 대화 Dialog

Learn vivid local expression using core grammar in the background of the theme travel destination.

맛있는 회화 TIP

Learn conversational tips to speak like a native.

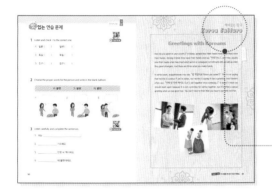

• 맛있는 연습 문제 Exercise

You can review the key points you learned today.

재미있는 한국 Korea Culture

You can learn about Korean culture.

• WEEK 다시 보기 Review

Summarize what you have learned during the week at a glance, and review it thoroughly with exercises.

맛으로 만나 보는 한국 Korea through taste

Explore local food that even the locals enjoy.

이렇게 말해요! Say like this!

Learn the special expressions that you must use at least once.

우리만 알고 있는 여행 이야기 The Travel Story that Only We Know

Let's find out the characteristics and hidden charms of each region of Korea together.

Introduce a special supplements to support self-taught!

• Special Supplements •

Workbook

Listening to the recording, you can write and practice Hangeul, dialogs and words.

Expression Mini-Book

It contains words and sentences that can be used directly in Korea.

South Korea map

You can meet today's travel destinations in advance with a map that allows you to see themed destinations at a glance.

Hangeul Keyboard

Cut off the keyboard trace and practice the typing and learn Hangeul.

Hangeul at a Glance

Consonants and Vowels are arranged to see easily.

Free MP3

It is recorded with the vivid pronunciation of native speakers, so it is easy to learn Korean.

MP3 File Download

You can download the QR code as soon as you scan it.

You can log in to the 맛있는books website (www. booksJRC.com) and download it on your PC.

Contents

Preface		003
How to Use This book		004
Special Supplements		006
Contents		008

Study Planner		010
About Korean language&Korea		012
Explanatory notes		014
Characters		015

WEEK 01 | 지금 서울을 만나러 가자! Let's go see Seoul now!

DAY 01 Learning Hangeul 1 — Consonants & Vowels | 018

DAY 02 Learning Hangeul 2 — Consonants & Vowels | 026

DAY 03 Learning Hangeul 3 — Vowels & Batchim | 034

DAY 04 Introducing — 이 사람은 제 친구 또안 씨예요. | 042
This is my friend, Mr. Doan. ◆ Incheon

DAY 05 First week Review | 052

WEEK 02 | 경기도? 강원도? 다 좋아요! Gyeonggi-do? Gangwon-do? All good!

DAY 06 Placing an order — 커피 한 잔 주세요. | 060
A cup of coffee, please. ◆ Dumulmeori

DAY 07 Speaking about possession — 교통 카드가 있어요? | 070
Do you have a transportation card? ◆ Heyri Art Valley

DAY 08 Explaining — 요즘도 한국어를 배워요? | 080
Are you still learning Korean these days? ◆ Sokcho

DAY 09 Describing — 한복이 정말 많아요. | 090
There are so many hanboks. ◆ Suwon

DAY 10 Second week Review | 100

WEEK 03 | 한국의 문화 도시로 떠나 볼까요? Shall we go to the cultural city of Korea?

DAY 11 Speaking about plans
친구들하고 파티를 할 거예요.
I will have a party with my friends.
| 108
◆ Danyang

DAY 12 Speaking about the past and hope
지난 주말에 머드 축제에 갔어요.
I went to the Mud Festival last weekend.
| 118
◆ Boryeong

DAY 13 Expressing the means
KTX로 가세요.
Go by KTX.
| 128
◆ Gyeongju

DAY 14 Making a suggestion
우리 좀 쉴까요?
Shall we take a rest?
| 138
◆ Jeonju

DAY 15 Third week Review
| 148

WEEK 04 | 한국의 관광 도시로 떠나요. Let's go to a tourist city in Korea.

DAY 16 Speaking in Determiner-form
정말 아름다운 곳이에요.
It's a really beautiful place.
| 156
◆ Daegu

DAY 17 Speaking about reason
그냥 심심해서 전화했어요.
I called just because I was bored.
| 166
◆ Ulsan

DAY 18 Expressing the conditions
안나가 오면 출발하자.
Let's go when Anna comes.
| 176
◆ Busan

DAY 19 Expressing the feelings
여기는 정말 예쁘네.
It's really pretty here.
| 186
◆ Jeju

DAY 20 Fourth week Review
| 196

Answer | 203

Basic Korean Sentence Patterns | 218

Hangeul Keyboard | 223

Study Planner

WEEK 01

DAY 01	DAY 02	DAY 03	DAY 04	DAY 05
Ⓜ pp. 18–25 Ⓦ pp. 2–5	Ⓜ pp. 26–33 Ⓦ pp. 6–10	Ⓜ pp. 34–41 Ⓦ pp. 10–11	Ⓜ pp. 42–51 Ⓦ pp. 12–13	Ⓜ pp. 52–57
Date /	Date /	Date /	Date /	Date /
Hangeul 1 • Consonants • Vowels	**Hangeul 2** • Consonants • Vowels	**Hangeul 3** • Vowels • Batchim	**Introducing** • 저는 N이에요/예요 • 이 N • 그 N, 저 N	**Review** DAY **01**–DAY **04**

WEEK 02

DAY 06	DAY 07	DAY 08	DAY 09	DAY 10
Ⓜ pp. 60–69 Ⓦ pp. 14–15	Ⓜ pp. 70–79 Ⓦ pp. 16–17	Ⓜ pp. 80–89 Ⓦ pp. 18–19	Ⓜ pp. 90–99 Ⓦ pp. 20–21	Ⓜ pp. 100–105
Date /	Date /	Date /	Date /	Date /
Placing an order • N입니다 • V–(으)세요	**Speaking about possession** • N이/가 있어요[없어요] • V–아요/어요 • N에서	**Explaining** • N에 • N도 • N을/를	**Describing** • N이/가 A–아요/어요 • 'ㅡ' drop out	**Review** DAY **06**–DAY **09**

Learn the basics of Korean in 20 days!

WEEK 03

DAY 11	**DAY 12**	**DAY 13**	**DAY 14**	**DAY 15**
Ⓜ pp. 108–117 Ⓦ pp. 22–23	Ⓜ pp. 118–127 Ⓦ pp. 24–25	Ⓜ pp. 128–137 Ⓦ pp. 26–27	Ⓜ pp. 138–147 Ⓦ pp. 28–29	Ⓜ pp. 148–153
Date /	Date /	Date /	Date /	Date /
Speaking about plans	**Speaking about the past and hope**	**Expressing the means**	**Making a suggestion**	**Review**
• V–(으)ㄹ 거예요 • N하고	• V/A–았어요/었어요 • V–고 싶다	• N(으)로 • 'ㅂ' irregular	• V–(으)ㄹ까요? • V–고	DAY **11**–DAY **14**

WEEK 04

DAY 16	**DAY 17**	**DAY 18**	**DAY 19**	**DAY 20**
Ⓜ pp. 156–165 Ⓦ pp. 30–31	Ⓜ pp. 166–175 Ⓦ pp. 32–33	Ⓜ pp. 176–185 Ⓦ pp. 34–35	Ⓜ pp. 186–195 Ⓦ pp. 36–37	Ⓜ pp. 196–201
Date /	Date /	Date /	Date /	Date /
Speaking in Determiner-form	**Speaking about reason**	**Expressing the conditions**	**Expressing the feelings**	**Review**
• A–(으)ㄴ / V–는 N • 안 V/A	• V/A–아서/어서 • V–고 있다	• Casual speech • V/A–(으)면	• V/A–네요 • 못 V	DAY **16**–DAY **19**

What Korean do we study?

*Korean

Having been used only in Korea, Korean is now being loved and used all over the world. As of October 2020, the number of people who speak Korean as a first language is about 77 million, and it is ranked 14th among the world's languages. As Hallyu such as Pop and K-drama become popular, Korean is getting more and more love.

*Hangeul

Korean characters are Hangeul, right? Hangeul, created during the Joseon Dynasty, is a scientific, original, and efficient script. Many scholars have praised that it has a more scientific system than any other script in the world. Currently, 19 consonants and 21 vowels are being used in Hangeul.

*Basic word order

The basic word order of Korean sentences is the 'subject-predicate' structure. Depending on the sentence, its structure may be expressed in the form of 'subject-object–predicate', 'subject–complement–predicate', or may include some adverbial complement.

저는 책을 읽어요. I read a book.
S   O   V

제 동생은 의사가 되었어요. My younger brother became a doctor.
    S   C   V

저는 학교에 가요. I go to school.
S   AC   V

What kind of country is Korea?

Area

Korea is a peninsula surrounded by sea on three sides. With an area of **106,210km²**, South Korea ranks 108th in the world.

Nation name

The official name of Korea is "**대한민국** (Republic of Korea)".

Population

According to the report of the National Statistical Office in 2021, the current population of South Korea is about **52 million**. It is the 28th most populous in the world.

Capital

The capital of South Korea is **Seoul**. Seoul is a special city where traditional beauty and modern beauty coexist.

Weather

Korea has relatively distinct four seasons. Spring is warm and summer is hot. It rains a lot in summer, and that time is called the "장마철(rainy season)". Autumn in Korea is cool and the sky is very clear. Winter is cold and snowy.

Travel Information

+ **Currency** : Won (KRW)
+ **Working voltage** : 220V
+ **Time to travel** : You can feel the beauty no matter what time of year you come.
+ Short-term trips to South Korea within **15 days** are mostly allowed **visa-free**. Please refer to the South Korean visa portal site (https://www.visa.go.kr/main/openMain.do).

Explanatory notes

1 For accurate pronunciation learning, please learn by listening to the actual pronunciation of the native speakers.

2 For the convenience of learning, the recording is done slightly slower than normal speed.

3 The conversation is structured by selecting words according to the level of learners who are learning Korean for the first step.

4 Korean grammar is explained to point out the core contents that can be learned easily and applied practically.

MP3 File Composition

본책
Main Book

맛있는 핵심 문법
Grammar

You can listen to all the examples in the main book's "맛있는 핵심 문법" and the complete sentences from "실력 다지기".

맛있는 대화
Dialog

Listening to the whole dialog → Listening (sentence by sentence)

표현 미니북
Expression Mini-Book

You can listen to the sentences and words that are highly useful in Korea.

쓰기 노트
Workbook

You can listen to the Korean consonants and vowels, dialogs, and words.

★ **MP3 File Download**

You can download it for free from the 맛있는books website (www.booksJRC.com).

Travel Route

WEEK 01
WEEK 02
WEEK 03
WEEK 04

- Sokcho
- Paju
- Seoul
- Incheon
- Yangpyeong
- Suwon
- Danyang
- Boryeong
- Jeonju
- Daegu
- Gyeongju
- Ulsan
- Busan
- Jejudo Island

Characters

피터
Peter

American, worker

윤기
Yoonki

Korean, worker

또안
Doan

Vietnamese, international student

민영
Minyoung

Korean, college student

안나
Anna

German, international student

지금 서울을 만나러 가자!
Let's go see Seoul now!

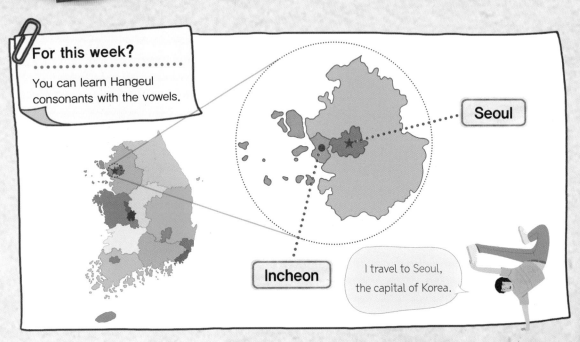

For this week?

You can learn Hangeul consonants with the vowels.

Seoul

Incheon

I travel to Seoul, the capital of Korea.

DAY 01

한글 배우기 1

Learning Hangeul

DAY 02

한글 배우기 2

Learning Hangeul

DAY 03   한글 배우기 3
Learning Hangeul

DAY 04   소개하기
Introducing

DAY 05

First week DAY 01–04 Review

Review the main lessons of DAY 01–04, and check your Korean with various questions.

Travel & Culture in Korea

Find out what Korea is like and the street food that represents Korea.

DAY 01

맛있는 한글 배우기 1
Learning Hangeul

You know Hangeul, the Korean alphabet?

Hangeul is the letter that was created by King Sejong the Great, King of Joseon Dynasty. King Sejong believed that the country would develop only if lives of those who could not read were improved. At that time, ordinary people often did not know the used letters because they were in Chinese characters. So, Hangeul was created over a long period of research for ordinary people. Hangeul is made up of consonants and vowels, and it is made in the following principles.

1 자음 Consonants

There are 19 consonants (ㄱ, ㄴ, ㄷ, ㄹ, …) in Hangeul. The consonants are modeled after the shape of human pronunciation organs (lips, tongue, throat). And some consonants were created by adding more strokes to the basic consonant as in 'ㄱ, ㄴ, ㅁ, ㅅ, ㅇ' (ㄱ → ㅋ, ㅅ → ㅈ) or by writing the same letter side by side (ㄱ → ㄲ, ㅅ → ㅆ).

articulation position	basic consonants	adding stroke		double consonants	special consonant
tongue shape blocking the throat by the root of tongue	ㄱ		ㅋ	ㄲ	
tongue shape touching the upper gums	ㄴ	ㄷ	ㅌ	ㄸ	ㄹ

18

articulation position	basic consonants	adding stroke		double consonants
shape of lips	ㅁ	ㅂ	ㅍ	ㅃ
shape of teeth	ㅅ	ㅈ	ㅊ	ㅆ ㅉ
shape of the throat	ㅇ		ㅎ	

Consonants in Hangeul have names.

ㄱ 기역	ㄴ 니은	ㄷ 디귿	ㄹ 리을	ㅁ 미음
ㅂ 비읍	ㅅ 시옷	ㅇ 이응	ㅈ 지읒	ㅊ 치읓
ㅋ 키읔	ㅌ 티읕	ㅍ 피읖	ㅎ 히읗	

② 모음 Vowels

There are 21 vowels (ㅏ, ㅓ, ㅗ, ㅡ, …) in Hanguel. They were made, based on the characteristics of the sky, the earth, and human. Making '·' was based on the characteristics of the sky around as they think, making 'ㅡ' on the usually flat earth, and making 'ㅣ' on the shape of a standing person. And 'ㅏ' was created by combining 'ㅣ' and '·' as the principle of synthesis.

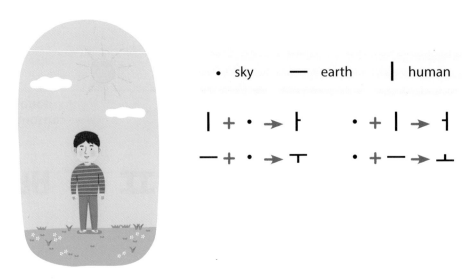

| • | sky | — | earth | | | human |

$$| + • \rightarrow \vdash \qquad • + | \rightarrow \dashv$$
$$— + • \rightarrow \top \qquad • + — \rightarrow \bot$$

The Korean vowels are as follows.

ㅏ	ㅑ	ㅓ	ㅕ	ㅗ	ㅛ	ㅜ
ㅠ	ㅡ	ㅣ	ㅐ	ㅒ	ㅔ	ㅖ
ㅘ	ㅝ	ㅟ	ㅢ	ㅚ	ㅙ	ㅞ

 3 글자 Letter

One letter is made of consonant and vowel.

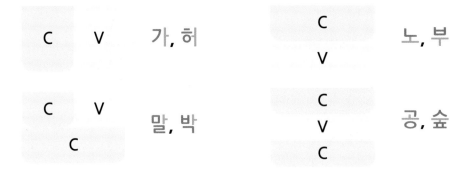

Hangeul made in this way has the advantage of expressing many sounds. After Hangeul was created, many people could read and write, and Joseon Dynasty developed further. Hangeul is a functional language that contains the warm heart of King Sejong who loved his people. They praised the scientific characteristics and the originality of principle in making the Hangeul letter for its excellence.

letter	ㅏ	ㅓ	ㅗ	ㅜ	ㅡ	ㅣ
sound	[a]	[ə]	[o]	[u]	[ɨ]	[i]

writing order	ㅏ	ㅓ	ㅗ	ㅜ	ㅡ	ㅣ

연습 Practice1 Listen carefully and read along.

아　　어　　오　　우　　으　　이

💡 **TIP** ∨ : For syllables that start with a vowel, 'ㅏ' alone cannot be used. You must write 'ㅇ' together in front of 'ㅏ'. In this case, 'ㅇ' plays the role of filling in the space without a sound to complete the character. Even a single vowel sound can be a word with meaning in Korean.

연습 Practice2 Listen carefully and read along.

오	이	오이	아이
five	two	cucumber	child

2 기본 자음 배우기 Learning the basic consonants

Track 01-02

letter	ㄱ	ㄴ	ㅁ	ㅅ	ㅇ
sound	[k/g]	[n]	[m]	[s]	[ø]
writing order	ㄱ	ㄴ	ㅁ	ㅅ	ㅇ

❄ **TIP** **C + V** : In Korean, consonants and vowels meet to form one letter. In this case, the consonant is written to the left or above the vowel. Image writing a syllabic letter inside a square box, the consonant and the vowel are written together.

━ 연습 Practice1 ━ Listen carefully and read along.

가	나	마	사	아
거	노	머	소	우

━ 연습 Practice2 ━ Listen carefully and read along.

가구	거미	나무	가수	어머니
furniture	spider	tree	singer	mother

❄ **TIP** The writing shape of 'ㄱ' changes into '가, 거' when a vowel comes to the right or '고, 구' when it to the bottom.

3 자음 더 배우기 Learning the more consonants

By adding more stroke to a consonant, another consonant was created.

letter	ㄷ	ㄹ	ㅂ	ㅈ	ㅎ
sound	[t/d]	[r/l]	[p/b]	[ʧ/j]	[h]
writing order	ㄷ	ㄹ	ㅂ	ㅈ	ㅎ

🔊 연습 Practice1 🔊 Listen carefully and read along.

다	라	바	자	하
더	루	보	지	호

🔊 연습 Practice2 🔊 Listen carefully and read along.

다리	바다	사자	나비	다리미
leg	sea	lion	butterfly	iron

있는 연습 문제

Track 01-04

1 Listen and check ∨ to the correct one.

① 아 (   )　　　어 (   )

② 오 (   )　　　우 (   )

③ 어 (   )　　　이 (   )

Track 01-05

2 Listen and check ∨ to the correct one.

① 가지 (   )　　　고지 (   )

② 고미 (   )　　　거미 (   )

③ 사자 (   )　　　서주 (   )

④ 너무 (   )　　　나무 (   )

 Track 01-06

3 Listen carefully and fill in the blank.

① _____이　　　　　　② _____이

③ 가_____　　　　　　④ 다_____

⑤ _____나　　　　　　⑥ 나_____

⑦ _____디오　　　　　⑧ 아_____지

24

The capital of Korea, Seoul

Seoul, the capital of Korea, is a beautiful city and has been the center of Korean politics, economy, culture and history since ancient times.

Although Seoul covers an area of 605㎢, it is a megalopolis were about 10,000,000 citizens are live and is growing as Asia's economic and cultural center.

Seoul is home to many venture companies such as apparel, pharmaceuticals, and electronics industries, as well as Namdaemun Market, Dongdaemun Market, Noryangjin Fish Market, and various department stores.

And are all located good medical facilities, best educational institutions, and various sports facilities in Seoul.

Seoul is the center of Korean culture, arts and tourism, with many things to see and do.

맛있는 한글 배우기 2
Learning Hangeul

1 **모음 배우기** Learning the vowels

Track 02-01

The following vowels were created by synthesizing the strokes of basic vowels.

letter	ㅑ	ㅕ	ㅛ	ㅠ
sound	[ya]	[yə]	[yo]	[yu]
writing order				

연습 Practice1 Listen carefully and read along.

야　　　여　　　요　　　유

연습 Practice2 Listen carefully and read along.

교수	우유	야구	요리	여자
professor	milk	baseball	cooking	woman

26

2 모음 더 배우기 Learning the more vowels

Track 02-02

The following vowels were created by synthesizing the strokes of basic vowels.

letter	ㅐ	ㅒ	ㅔ	ㅖ
sound	[ɛ]	[yɛ]	[e]	[ye]
writing order				

🌀 **TIP** 'ㅐ' and 'ㅔ' are very similar in pronunciation. So are 'ㅒ' and 'ㅖ'. However, since they can show differences as in '게(crab)' and '개(dog)', it is better to study the vowels with words rather than only to study them.

연습 Practice1 Listen carefully and read along.

애   얘   에   예

연습 Practice2 Listen carefully and read along.

게	배	새	세수	시계
crab	ship	bird	washing one's face	clock

3 자음 배우기 Learning the consonants

Track 02-03

By adding more stroke to a consonant, another consonant was created.

letter	ㅋ	ㅌ	ㅍ	ㅊ
sound	[k^h]	[t^h]	[p^h]	[ʧ^h]
writing order	ㅋ	ㅌ	ㅍ	ㅊ

TIP 'ㅋ, ㅌ, ㅍ, ㅊ' are pronounced by expelling air harder than 'ㄱ, ㄷ, ㅂ, ㅈ'.

연습 Practice1 ▶ Listen carefully and read along.

카 　 타 　 파 　 차

연습 Practice2 ▶ Listen carefully and read along.

기타	커피	피자	해파리	케이크
guitar	coffee	pizza	jellyfish	cake

Another consonant was created by writing the same letter side by side.

letter	ㄲ	ㄸ	ㅃ	ㅆ	ㅉ
sound	[k']	[t']	[p']	[s']	[ʧ']
writing order	ㄲ	ㄸ	ㅃ	ㅆ	ㅉ

💮 **TIP** These consonants are pronounced more strongly than 'ㄱ, ㄷ, ㅂ, ㅅ, ㅈ' by being given more strength to the throat and stomach when we pronounce them.

연습 Practice1 Listen carefully and read along.

까　　따　　빠　　싸　　짜

연습 Practice2 Listen carefully and read along.

오빠	토끼	꼬리	아저씨	코끼리
elder/older brother	rabbit	tail	middle-aged man	elephant

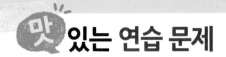 있는 연습 문제

1 Listen and check V to the correct one.

 Track 02-05

① 어 (   )   여 (   )   ② 오 (   )   유 (   )

③ 아 (   )   요 (   )   ④ 요 (   )   유 (   )

⑤ 에 (   )   예 (   )   ⑥ 얘 (   )   애 (   )

⑦ 여 (   )   예 (   )   ⑧ 야 (   )   에 (   )

⑨ 가 (   )   카 (   )   ⑩ 도 (   )   토 (   )

⑪ 부 (   )   푸 (   )   ⑫ 자 (   )   차 (   )

2 Listen carefully and fill in the blank.

 Track 02-06

① _____구   ② _____리

③ _____수   ④ 시_____

⑤ _____피   ⑥ _____이크

⑦ 아_____   ⑧ 코_____리

3 Listen carefully and read along.

Track 02-07

오리 duck	타조 ostrich	하마 hippo	토끼 rabbit	너구리 raccoon
가지 eggplant	바나나 banana	고구마 sweet potato	체리 cherry	포도 grape
바구니 basket	카드 card	비누 soap	휴지 toilet paper	지우개 eraser
피아노 piano	기타 guitar	하모니카 harmonica	마이크 microphone	노래 song
코트 coat	치마 skirt	바지 pants	티셔츠 T-shirt	구두 shoes

맛있는 한국어 인사 한마디 Useful Korean greeting word

Track 02-08

1

안녕하세요?
Hello..

안녕하세요?
Hello.

2

안녕?
Hi.

안녕?
Hi.

3

감사합니다. / 고맙습니다.
Thank you.

4

고마워.
Thanks.

5

죄송합니다.
Sorry.

6

미안해.
Sorry.

7

안녕히 가세요.
Goodbye.

안녕히 계세요.
Goodbye.

8

잘 가.
Bye.

잘 있어.
Bye.

Beautiful Seoul

As a representative tourist destination in Seoul, many people visit Namsan Mountain.
There is N Seoul Tower on the Mountain, and you can see as far as Incheon on a clear day.

Namsan Mountain is famous as a place that has appeared many times in dramas. In particular, it is renowned as a dating course for lovers as there are many places where you can hang a love lock, which means that it promises eternal love. It's a great place to make memories with your loved ones, even if you're not in a romantic relationship.

The view of Seoul at night is even more attractive. Hangang Park is a great place to enjoy the night view. It consists of 11 parks along the Hangang River, including Ttukseom, Banpo, and Yeouido. It will be fun to feel the characteristics of each park. There are also places where you can ride a bike or take a walk, and some have an outdoor swimming pool in summer, so it's a good idea to go there after checking in advance.
Chimaek, fried chicken and beer, which you can enjoy leisurely on the Hangang River Side, will be another memorable experience. Go to the Hangang River and enjoy the specialness of Korea's delivery culture, which brings the delivery (Chimaek) to the Hangang Park.

맛있는 한글 배우기 3
Learning Hangeul

1 모음 배우기 Learning the vowels

Track 03-01

The following vowels were created by synthesizing the strokes of basic vowels.

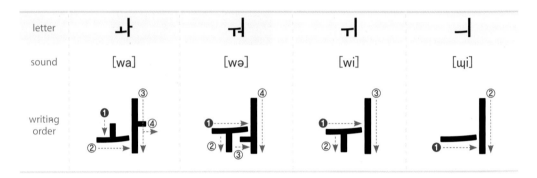

letter	ㅘ	ㅝ	ㅟ	ㅢ
sound	[wa]	[wə]	[wi]	[ɰi]

💡 **TIP** In the pronunciation of the vowel, think of pronouncing 'ㅗ+ㅏ', 'ㅜ+ㅓ', 'ㅜ+ㅣ' or 'ㅡ+ㅣ' quickly at a time, and then practice it!

🔊 연습 Practice1 ▶ Listen carefully and read along.

와　　　워　　　위　　　의

🔊 연습 Practice2 ▶ Listen carefully and read along.

귀	사과	키위	의사	의자
ear	apple	kiwi	doctor	chair

2 모음 더 배우기 Learning the more vowels

Track 03-02

The following vowels were created by synthesizing the strokes of basic vowels.

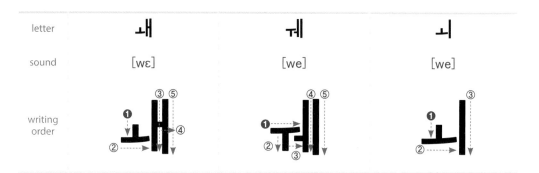

letter	ㅙ	ㅞ	ㅚ
sound	[wɛ]	[we]	[we]
writing order			

☀ **TIP** The pronunciation of these vowels is so similar one another that even Koreans can't tell them apart. It is better to study with words rather than study only vowels.

🔊 연습 Practice1 🔊 Listen carefully and read along.

왜　　웨　　외

🔊 연습 Practice2 🔊 Listen carefully and read along.

왜	돼지	회사	스웨터	웨이터
why	pig	company	sweater	waiter

3 받침 배우기 Learning Batchim(Base)

letter	ㄱ,ㅋ,ㄲ	ㄴ	ㄷ,ㅌ, ㅅ,ㅆ, ㅈ,ㅊ,ㅎ	ㄹ	ㅁ	ㅂ,ㅍ	ㅇ
sound	[k]	[n]	[t]	[l]	[m]	[p]	[ŋ]
	악, 앜, 앆	안	앋, 앝, 앗, 았, 앚, 앛, 앟	알	암	압, 앞	앙

TIP C+V : Consonants can make up the Batchim(Base) of a Hangeul syllabic letter. However, it is pronounced
C(Batchim/Base) in seven tones like 'ㄱ, ㄴ, ㄷ, ㄹ, ㅁ, ㅂ, ㅇ'.

연습 Practice1 ▶ Listen carefully and read along.

각 　 간 　 갓 　 갈 　 감 　 갑 　 강

연습 Practice2 ▶ Listen carefully and read along.

[ㄱ]	박	밖	부엌	수박	악기
	gourd	outside	kitchen	watermelon	instrument

[ㄴ]	눈	돈	우산	친구	자전거
	snow	money	umbrella	friend	bicycle

[ㄷ]	옷	빗	낮	꽃	밑
	clothes	comb	daytime	flower	under

[ㄹ]	물	달	별	연필	딸기
	water	moon	star	pencil	strawberry

[ㅁ]	곰	삼	감	엄마	남자
	bear	three	persimmon	mom	man

[ㅂ]	밥	집	잎	숲	무릎
	meal	house	leaf	forest	knee

[ㅇ]	강	빵	가방	사랑	운동장
	river	bread	bag	love	playground

TIP There are also double final consonants where the Batchim(Base) has two consonants. In the double final consonants, only one consonant is sounded, not the both. Therefore, it is read in just one of the two base consonants.

닭[닥]	값[갑]	삶[삼]	몫[목]	여덟[여덜]
chicken	value	life	share	eight

읽다[익따]	없다[업따]	앉다[안따]	넓다[널따]
read	nothing	sit	wide

한국어의 특징 Characteristics of Korean

1 Korean is a language where post-position has been developed. A postposition is usually attached right after a noun to show the noun's role in the sentence. That is, it indicates whether a noun is a subject, an object, or a complement. Without postposition, it's difficult to convey exactly what you're trying to say, and if it is misused, it can lead to misunderstandings. So, when studying Korean words, it is recommended to study the postposition together like 'N에 가요(I go to N), N을/를 좋아해요(I like N)'.

2 The order of basic sentences in Korean is '**subject – predicate**', '**subject – object – predicate**', and '**subject – complement – predicate**'. It is a great feature that the object comes before its predicate. The subject, object or complement always has its own post-position as follows.

ex 저는 한국어를 배워요. I learn Korean language.
    S   O   V

제 동생은 선생님이 되었어요. My younger brother became a teacher.
    S   C   V

Track 03-04

3 A verb indicates its action and an adjective the status.
Shall we take a look at the basic verbs in Korean?

일어나다	세수하다	먹다	운동하다	공부하다
wake up	wash up	eat	exercise	study

일하다	전화하다	쇼핑하다	만나다	읽다
work	call	go shopping	meet	read

Shall we take a look at the basic adjectives in Korean?

싸다	비싸다	맛있다	맛없다	좋다
cheap	expensive	delicious	tasteless	good

따뜻하다	시원하다	재미있다	재미없다	깨끗하다
warm	cool	fun	boring	clean

A verb or adjective in Korean completes the sentence in the place of the predicate, at the end. To express what the speaker is trying to say, we need to attach a conjugated form to the basic stem of a verb(ex: 자다 sleep) or an adjective(ex: 좋다 good).

basic form	tense expression			expression of hope	expression of command
	past	present	future		
가다	갔어요	가요	갈 거예요	가고 싶어요	가세요
go	went	go	will go	want to go	go please

4 Honorifics are highly developed in Korean language. You may speak in honorific or casual speech to a person depending on your intimacy with the person.

할아버지, 주무세요?
Grandfather, are you sleeping?

지금 자요?
Are you sleeping now?

자?
Sleeping?

맛 있는 연습 문제

1 Listen and check V to the correct one.

 Track 03-06

① 아 (　　　) 와 (　　　)　　② 워 (　　　) 위 (　　　)

③ 위 (　　　) 의 (　　　)　　④ 와 (　　　) 왜 (　　　)

⑤ 웨 (　　　) 애 (　　　)　　⑥ 외 (　　　) 예 (　　　)

⑦ 곰 (　　　) 공 (　　　)　　⑧ 밥 (　　　) 박 (　　　)

⑨ 달 (　　　) 단 (　　　)　　⑩ 문 (　　　) 물 (　　　)

2 Read the following numbers.

 Track 03-07

일	이	삼	사	오	육
one	two	three	four	five	six
1	**2**	**3**	**4**	**5**	**6**

칠	팔	구	십	십일	십이
seven	eight	nine	ten	eleven	twelve
7	**8**	**9**	**10**	**11**	**12**

이십	삼십	사십	오십	백	이백
twenty	thirty	forty	fifty	one hundred	two hundred
20	**30**	**40**	**50**	**100**	**200**

KOREA

A special street in Seoul

There are many cafes and restaurants in Seoul, such as Garosu-gil and Hongdae Street near Hongik University.

Among them, Ikseon-dong, Jongno-gu, is one of the recently attracted attention.

Ikseon-dong is a place where hanoks built in the 1920s remain. Many hanoks there have been reborn as cafes. These many hanok cafes have unique feelings compared to other cafes, and lots of people visit the hanok-cafes to take pictures there.

Itaewon is one of the most visited places by foreigners. It is a place where you can taste food from various countries, and it is a place frequented by foreigners living in Korea. There are many popular restaurants and cafes with a special atmosphere to have an extraordinary experience there.

Gwangjang Market is famous for its food. Since it is a market, they sell a lot of easy-to-eat food (tteokbokki, gimbap, and bindaetteok). Among them, Bindaetteok is a food loved by many foreign tourists.

Ikseon-dong

Gwangjang Market

Itaewon

이 사람은 제 친구 또안 씨예요.

This is my friend, Mr. Doan.

 지난 학습 **다시 보기 Review**

- Hangeul is composed of consonants and vowels:

    Consonant(C)s - There are ㄱ–ㅋ–ㄲ, ㄷ–ㅌ–ㄸ etc.

    Vowel(V)s - There are ㅏ, ㅑ, ㅓ, ㅕ etc.

- A Korean syllable consists of V, C+V, and C+V+C.

    ⓔⓧ 아이 child, 가수 singer, 선생님 teacher

- The ending of the descriptive words changes in Korean.

    ⓔⓧ 가요 go, 가고 싶어요 want to go

- Postposition and honorific are highly specific in Korean.

    ⓔⓧ 저는 밥을 먹어요. I eat rice.

    할아버지는 신문을 읽으세요. Grandpa reads the newspaper.

 학습 포인트 Point

✫ Learn the expressions to introduce or explain.

✫ Learn the expressions to direct things.

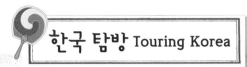

Welcome! Welcome to Korea. Maybe there are many people who may have arrived at Incheon International Airport. The Airport is very famous as you know or will know. The size is big, but the transportation is convenient and the service is good, such as subway, airport bus and taxi. There are many good restaurants there around. If you haven't decided where to go on the first day of arriving in Korea, how about stopping by a popular restaurant at Incheon International Airport Terminal 2 to have a meal at first?

In Incheon, where Incheon Airport is located, there are famous places such as Wolmido Island, Songwol-dong Donghwa Village, and Chinatown. Because Incheon is close to Seoul, the capital of Korea, as well as the West Sea, lots of people often visit there.

Wolmido Island has many places where you can eat saengseonhoe(sashimi), while looking at the sea. Songwol-dong Donghwa Village is a place where you can see cute images as if you are coming into a fairy tale. Famous tourist attractions in Korea such as Seoul, Busan, and Jejudo Island are very good, but it would be nice to look around in Incheon as well.

Sentence
핵심 문장

01 저는 이윤기예요.
I'm Lee Yoonki.

02 이 사람은 제 친구 또안 씨예요.
This is my friend, Mr. Doan.

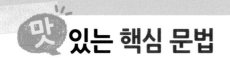

01 저는 이윤기예요.
I'm Lee Yoonki.

✓ 저는 N이에요/예요

	N		이에요/예요
Batchim O	또안	Doan	저는 또안이에요. I'm Doan.
Batchim X	이윤기	Lee Yoonki	저는 이윤기예요. I'm Lee Yoonki.

'이에요/예요' comes right after a noun to predicate its attribute or the class. '저는 N이에요/예요' can be used to introduce myself politely. In this case, you can use a noun that represents your name, nationality, occupation, etc.

ex When speaking the nationality

한국 사람 Korean
베트남 사람 Vietnamese
미국 사람 American   + 이에요
태국 사람 Thai
러시아 사람 Russian
중국 사람 Chinese

저는 한국 사람이에요. I'm Korean.
저는 독일 사람이에요. I'm German.

ex When indicating a job

회사원 office worker
선생님 teacher   + 이에요
학생 student

기자 reporter
의사 doctor   + 예요
요리사 cook

저는 회사원이에요. I'm an office worker.
저는 기자예요. I'm a reporter.

TIP When it comes to nationality, you have to say, "저는 [country name] 사람이에요." '저는 한국이에요.' is an awkward expression. '(N)은/는' in '저는' indicates that N(저) becomes the subject or the topic of sentence.

단어 Vocabulary

저 I
태국 Thailand
독일 Germany

한국 Korea
러시아 Russia

베트남 Vietnam
중국 China

미국 the United States
사람 person

실력 다지기 Practice1

▶ Change the following words and fill in the blank.

	N이에요/예요
일본 사람	일본 사람이에요
가수	
친구	
학생	

실력 다지기 Practice2

▶ Practice the following as in |ex|.

| ex |
한국 사람 → 저는 한국 사람이에요.

① 의사 → 저는 _____

② 베트남 사람 → 저는 _____

③ 회사원 → _____

④ 요리사 → _____

⑤ 중국 사람 → _____

⑥ 선생님 → _____

⑦ 배우 → _____

단어 Vocabulary

일본 Japan   가수 singer   친구 friend   배우 actor

02 이 사람은 제 친구 또안 씨예요.

This is my friend, Mr. Doan.

✓ 이 N

'이 N' is used to point to an object close to the speaker.

ex 이 가방은 제 가방이에요. This bag is mine.

✓ 그 N, 저 N

Use '그' to point to an object close to the listener, and '저' to point to something far away from both the speaker and the listener.

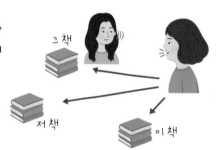

ex 그 사람은 제 친구예요. The person near you is my friend.
저 사람은 누구예요? Who is that person (over there)?

You can also use one of them in the form of a pronoun '이거, 그거' or '저거' when you refer to an object.

ex 이거는 제 가방이에요. This is my bag.
그거는 제 볼펜이에요. That's my ballpoint pen.
저거는 제 책이에요. That's my book.

💡 **TIP** 이 가방은 제 가방이에요: 'N은/는' represents that N is the subject, topic of the sentence. Use '은' right after a noun with a Batchim and '는' after a noun without a Batchim.

💡 **TIP** 저 사람은 누구예요?: If you raise the intonation of 'N이에요/예요', it means a question.
ex 이거는 가방이에요? (↗) Is this a bag?

단어 Vocabulary

가방 bag	제 my	누구 who	이거 this
그거 that (near you)	저거 that (over there)	볼펜 ballpoint pen	책 book

◖ 실력 다지기 Practice3 ◗

▶ Practice the following as in |ex|.

|ex| **이 사람 / 선생님** → 이 사람은 선생님이에요.

① 그 사람 / 의사   → _____

② 저 사람 / 가수   → _____

③ 이 책 / 제 책   → _____

④ 이 볼펜 / 윤기 씨 볼펜   → _____

◖ 실력 다지기 Practice4 ◗

▶ Practice the following as in |ex|.

|ex| **이거 / 제 가방** → 이거는 제 가방이에요.

① 저거 / 또안 씨 책   → _____

② 이거 / 볼펜   → _____

③ 그거 / 바나나   → _____

✿ **TIP** 윤기 씨 볼펜: When you use '의' to express possession in Korean, it is called '윤기 씨의 볼펜(Yoonki's ballpoint pen)' for example, but you can say '윤기 씨 볼펜' by omitting '의' when you usually speak.

💬 **단어** Vocabulary

씨 Mr, Ms   바나나 banana

 **있는 대화**

 Track 04-07

☀ 윤기와 또안이 처음 만났습니다.

피터	윤기 씨, 이 사람은 제 친구 또안 씨예요.

윤기   안녕하세요? 저는 이윤기예요.① 만나서 반가워요.②

또안   안녕하세요? 저는 또안이에요.

　　　저는 베트남 사람이에요.

단어 Vocabulary

사람 person
제 my
친구 friend
만나다 meet
반갑다 Nice to meet you
베트남 Vietnam

🗨 Summarize the dialog

① 또안 씨는 피터 씨의 ＿＿＿＿＿＿＿＿＿예요.

② 또안 씨는 ＿＿＿＿＿＿＿＿＿ 사람이에요.

☀ Yoonki and Doan met for the first time.

Peter Mr. Yoonki, this is my friend, Mr. Doan.

Yoonki Hello, I'm Lee Yoonki. Nice to meet you.

Doan Hello, I'm Doan.
I'm Vietnamese.

 맛있는 대화 TIP

① Korean's name is consist of 'last name+first name'. When we call Koreans, we usually call
'이윤기 씨(Mr. Lee Yoonki)' or '윤기 씨(Mr. Yoonki: You can think Lee is just omitted here.)'.
Don't call me '이 씨(Mr. Lee)'. Like in '이 과장님(Manager Lee)' or '김 선생님(Teacher Kim)', the
calling is according to the position, or depending on the age like in '윤기 형(Brother Yoonki)'
or '민영 언니(Sister Minyoung)'.

② '만나서 반가워요.(Nice to meet you.)' is often used as a greeting when we first meet.

맛있는 연습 문제

Track 04-08

1 Listen and check V to the correct one.

① 일본 (　　　)　　　일번 (　　　)

② 독길 (　　　)　　　독일 (　　　)

③ 친구 (　　　)　　　침구 (　　　)

2 Choose the proper words for the picture and write in the blank balloon.

| 이 볼펜 | 그 볼펜 | 저 볼펜 |

3 Listen carefully and complete the sentences.

Track 04-09

① 저는 _____.

② _____ 가수예요.

③ _____ 민영 씨 책이에요.

④ _____ 제 볼펜이에요.

Greetings with Koreans

How do you greet in your country? In Korea, people bow their heads more often than wave their hands. Among friends they wave their hands and say "안녕?(Hi.)", but they usually bow their heads when they meet adult senior or colleagues not intimate with as well as when they greet strangers. And there are times when you shake hands.

In some cases, acquaintances may say, "밥 먹었어요?(Have you eaten?)" This is not saying that he/she is curious if you've eaten, but he/she is saying it like a greeting. And Koreans often say, "언제 밥 한번 먹어요.(Let's eat together once someday.)" It doesn't mean we should meet again because it is not a promise for eating together, but it's often a casual greeting when we say good-bye. You don't have to think that you have to eat with him/her.

첫째 주 다시 보기 DAY 01-04

First week Review

DAY 01-03

1. 모음 Vowels

ㅏ	ㅑ	ㅓ	ㅕ	ㅗ	ㅛ	ㅜ
ㅠ	ㅡ	ㅣ	ㅐ	ㅒ	ㅔ	ㅖ
ㅘ	ㅝ	ㅟ	ㅢ	ㅚ	ㅙ	ㅞ

2. 자음 Consonants

ㄱ	ㄲ	ㄴ	ㄷ	ㄸ	ㄹ	ㅁ
ㅂ	ㅃ	ㅅ	ㅆ	ㅇ	ㅈ	ㅉ
ㅊ	ㅋ	ㅍ	ㅌ	ㅎ		

3. 한국어의 음절 Korean syllables

① V: 이 two, 우유 milk

② C+V: 나 I, 거미 spider, 이사 move, 고기 meat

③ C+V+C: 밥 meal, 강 river, 밖 outside, 곰 bear, 연필 pencil, 자전거 bicycle

④ C+V+C(double Batchim/Base): 값 value, 닭 chicken, 읽다 read

52

실력 다지기 Practice1

1 Listen carefully and fill in the blank.

Track 05-01

① _____스   ② _____드

③ _____마   ④ 토_____토

⑤ _____지   ⑥ 지우_____

⑦ _____기   ⑧ _____기

⑨ _____자   ⑩ 운_____장

2 Listen carefully and read along.

Track 05-02

냉장고	컴퓨터	휴대 전화	노트북	의자
refrigerator	computer	cell phone	laptop	chair

책상	지갑	공책	필통	카메라
desk	wallet	notebook	pencil case	camera

거울	명함	우산	안경	사진
mirror	business card	umbrella	glasses	photo

◆ **한국어의 특징** Characteristics of Korean

① Post-position is highly developed in Korean language.

② The order of basic sentences in Korean is 'subject – predicate', 'subject – object – predicate' or 'subject – complement – predicate'. It is a great feature that the object comes before its predicate.

③ A verb indicates its action and an adjective the status. A verb or adjective in Korean completes its sentence in the place of the predicate, at the end. To express what the speaker is trying to say, there are various conjugated forms to choose to attach to the basic stem of a verb(ex: 자다 sleep) or an adjective(ex: 좋다 good).

④ Honorifics are highly developed in Korean language. You may speak in honorific or casual speech to a person depending on your intimacy with the person.

DAY 04

◆ **저는 N이에요/예요** ▶ This is an expression when I use to introduce myself. You can use it to say your name, nationality, or occupation.

> **ex** 저는 이윤기예요. I'm Lee Yoonki.
>
> 저는 한국 사람이에요. I'm Korean.
>
> 저는 한국어 선생님이에요. I'm a Korean teacher.

◆ **이 N, 그 N, 저 N** ▶ You can use one of them when referring to a noun. Use '그(that)' to point to an object close to the listener, and '저(that over there)' to point to something far away from both the speaker and the listener.

> **ex** 이 가방은 제 가방이에요. This bag is mine.
>
> 그 책은 윤기 씨 책이에요. That book is Yoonki's book.
>
> 저 사람은 누구예요? Who is that person (over there)?

파이팅!

실력 다지기 Practice2

1 Connect the following words to form a sentence.

① 저 / 안나 ▷ _____

② 이 사람 / 피터 씨 ▷ _____

③ 그 친구 / 태국 사람 ▷ _____

④ 저 책 / 안나 씨 책 ▷ _____

2 Listen carefully and choose the correct answer to the question. Track 05-03

① 가 고마워요.

　나 안녕하세요.

　다 안녕히 가세요.

② 가 한국이에요.

　나 제 책이에요.

　다 미국 사람이에요.

3 Choose the appropriate expression to fill in the blank.

① _____ 가방은 피터 씨 가방이에요.

　가 그 　　　　　　　　　　나 그거

② 이 사람은 _____ 친구 또안 씨예요.

　가 이 　　　　　　　　　　나 제

4 Look at the following sentences and try to find the mistake and correct them.

① 저는 프랑스예요. ▷ _____

② 그 사람은 중국 사람이예요. ▷ _____

*단어 Vocabulary　어느 which　나라 country　프랑스 France

우리만 알고 있는

여행 이야기

The Travel Story that Only We Know

📷 Welcome to Korea!

Korea has many mountains in the east with its high topography, and many plains in the west with the low topography. And you can enjoy the beautiful sea, for it is surrounded by the sea on three sides. Each sea is called the West Sea, the East Sea, and the South Sea. In the West Sea, you can see the big difference between the high and low tides, for the tidal flats are widely developed, and it is deep as well as clear in the East Sea. In the South Sea there are more than 2,000 islands, so the scenery is very beautiful.

Based on the natural topographies Korea region is classified into the central and the southern region.

The central region refers to Seoul, Incheon, Gyeonggi-do, and Chungcheong-do, Gangwon-do, while the southern regions refer to Jeolla-do, Gyeongsang-do, Busan Metropolitan City, and Jeju-do.

Administrative districts in Korea are divided into Seoul Special Metropolitan City and the six metropolitan cities including Incheon, Daejeon, Daegu, Gwangju, Busan and Ulsan, as well as Sejong Special Self-Governing City, Gyeonggi-do, Chungcheong-do, Jeolla-do, Gyeongsang-do, and Jeju Special Self-Governing Province.

Seoul, the capital of Korea, is the center of shopping, culture and art, and is a wonderful city where tradition and modernity blend together.

If you go to Gyeongbokgung Palace, Changdeokgung Palace, and Deoksugung Palace, you can feel the Korean tradition, and if you go to Dongdaemun DDP, you can feel the beauty of modern architecture.

Incheon Airport is not the only famous place in Incheon, for the city is close to Seoul and is overlooking the West Sea. Incheon also has Chinatown, where you can taste Chinese food, and Naengmyeon (Korean cold noodles) Street, where you can enjoy Naengmyeon, one of Korea's representative dishes. You can enjoy various water leisure activities at Songdo Central Park, the first seawater park in Korea.

맛으로
만나 보는
한국

Korea through taste

There are a lot of delicious foods in Korea, but I will introduce the representative foods that you can taste on the street.

🏅 떡볶이 Tteokbokki

Korean people's most favorite national snack! I cook a rice cake by frying in red pepper paste, but it is not difficult to cook, so I cook it a lot at home. It is a typical snack often found on the streets of Korea. It's spicy, but it tastes best by relieving all the stress!

🏅 붕어빵과 호떡 Bungeoppang and Hotteok

If you travel to Korea in winter, it is a street food you must try at least once. Bungeoppang is a fish-shaped bread with red beans inside. Once you taste its sweetness, you will never forget it.

Hotteok is a snack fried with sugar in a dough made of wheat grain, and is especially popular in winter. It's so sweet and delicious, and is the best taste that everyone loves.

이렇게 말해요! **Say like this!**

Say something like this when you eat delicious food.

정말 맛있네요!
It's really delicious!

WEEK 02

DAY 06-10

경기도? 강원도? 다 좋아요!
Gyeonggi-do? Gangwon-do? All good!

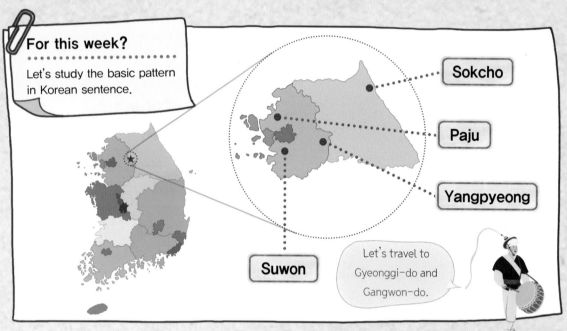

For this week?

Let's study the basic pattern in Korean sentence.

Sokcho

Paju

Yangpyeong

Suwon

Let's travel to Gyeonggi-do and Gangwon-do.

DAY 06 — 주문하기

Placing an order

DAY 07 — 소유 말하기

Speaking about possession

DAY 08 설명하기
Explaining

DAY 09 서술하기
Describing

DAY 10

Second week DAY 06–09 Review

Review the main lessons of DAY 06–09, and check your Korean with various questions.

Travel & Culture in Korea

Explore the major tourist attractions of Gyeonggi-do and Gangwon-do, and learn about Gangwon-do's representative food.

DAY 06

커피 한 잔 주세요.

A cup of coffee, please.

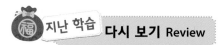

지난 학습 **다시 보기 Review**

◆ **저는 이윤기예요.**
I'm Lee Yoonki.

'N이에요/예요' is used to describe properties and attributes.

◆ **이 사람은 제 친구 또안 씨예요.**
This is my friend, Mr. Doan.

'이' comes before a noun and used when referring to an object close to the speaker, '그' is used to refer to an object close to the listener, and '저' is used to refer to an object far away from the both.

◆ Look at the following and answer O if it is correct or X if incorrect.

① 저는 윤기예요.　　　(　　　)

② 이 책은 제 책이에요.　　(　　　)

③ 저는 학생이예요.　　　(　　　)

Point

학습 포인트

☆ Learn expressions to say prices.

☆ Learn expressions to command and request.

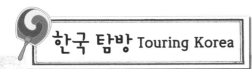

There are also many places to visit in Gyeonggi-do close to Seoul. Dumulmeori in Yangpyeong, where you can see the beautiful scenery, is also famous as a filming site for a drama. It is the starting point of the Hangang River, and is a good place to take a leisurely walk or take pictures. If you go to Dumulmeori, you can see a zelkova tree that is over 400 years old, and you can enjoy delicious hot dogs. So you should try to go for it.

Sentence 핵심 문장

03 **5,000원입니다.**
It is 5,000 won.

04 **커피 한 잔 주세요.**
A cup of coffee, please.

Track 06-01

03

5,000원입니다.

It is 5,000 won.

✓ N입니다

'입니다' comes right after a noun to predicate its attribute or the class.

	N		입니다
Batchim O	또안	Doan	또안입니다. I'm Doan.
Batchim X	이윤기	Lee Yoonki	이윤기입니다. I'm Lee Yoonki.

'N입니다' is used more officially or formally than 'N이에요/예요'. In the case, a noun can be used in indicating a name, nationality, occupation, and so on as well as in expressing the price of a product.

> **ex** 저는 안나입니다. 대학생입니다. I am Anna. I am a college student.
> 제 친구는 베트남 사람입니다. My friend is Vietnamese.

⚙ **TIP** When talking to a store worker, I say 'N입니다' a lot because I am usually not intimate with him/her.

⚙ **TIP** For reading numbers, see page 40.

100원	200원	300원	400원	500원	600원
백 원	이백 원	삼백 원	사백 원	오백 원	육백 원
700원	800원	900원	1,000원	2,000원	3,000원
칠백 원	팔백 원	구백 원	천 원	이천 원	삼천 원
4,000원	5,000원	10,000원	20,000원	50,000원	100,000원
사천 원	오천 원	만 원	이만 원	오만 원	십만 원

⚙ **TIP** 4,500 won is read as '사천오백 원(four thousand five hundred won)'.
25,000 won should be said to be '이만 오천 원(twenty-five thousand won)'.

만	천	백	십	
			90	원
		3	00	원
	6	0	00	원
5	0	0	00	원

⚙ **TIP** 10,000 won is not read as '일만 원', but '만 원'. 210,000 won should be said to be '이십일만 원'.

단어 Vocabulary

대학생 college student   원 won(Korean currency)

Track 06-02

━● 실력 다지기 Practice1 ●━

▶ Change the following words and fill in the blank.

	N입니다
일본 사람	일본 사람입니다
가수	
친구	
학생	

▶ How much is it? Try reading the price.

2,000원	이천 원	12,500원	
4,500원		54,000원	
7,600원		109,800원	

Track 06-03

━● 실력 다지기 Practice2 ●━

▶ Practice the following as in |ex|.

> |ex| **저 / 한국 사람** → 저는 한국 사람입니다.

① 제 친구 / 독일 사람 → _____

② 저 사람 / 회사원 → _____

③ 제 동생 / 대학생 → _____

④ 이윤기 씨 / 한국어 선생님 → _____

단어 Vocabulary

동생 younger brother/sister   한국어 Korean (language)

04

커피 한 잔 주세요.

A cup of coffee, please.

✓ V–(으)세요

'–(으)세요' is used with a verb to request or command for an action of the verb politely.

	basic form	–(으)세요
Batchim O	읽다 read	읽으세요 Please read
Batchim X	가다 go	가세요 Please go

ex 청소하세요. Clean it, please.　　　　나중에 전화하세요. Call me later, please.

비빔밥 하나 주세요. One bibimbap, please.

When you give a command politely that prohibits someone from doing something, you say 'V–지 마세요'.

ex 여기 오지 마세요. Don't come here.　　　　그 영화 보지 마세요. Don't watch that movie.

⚙ **TIP** When counting items in Korean, do the following.

1	2	3	4	5	6
하나	둘	셋	넷	다섯	여섯
7	8	9	10	20	30
일곱	여덟	아홉	열	스물	서른

⚙ **TIP** Use a unit noun(잔[cup], 병[bottle], 개[unit to count all nouns for object], 명[unit to count people], etc.) together when you count things. At this time, the counting numbers are changed before the noun like following: '하나 → 한, 둘 → 두, 셋 → 세, 넷 → 네'

ex　　커피 한 잔　　　　　　물 두 병　　　　　　가방 세 개　　　　　　친구 네 명

　　a cup of coffee　　two bottles of water　　three bags　　four friends

단어 Vocabulary

청소하다 clean　　　　나중 later　　　　전화하다 call　　　　비빔밥 bibimbap

주다 give　　　　　　여기 here　　　　오다 come　　　　　영화 movie

보다 watch, see　　　커피 coffee　　　물 water

64

■ 실력 다지기 Practice3

▶ Change the following words and fill in the blank.

	V-(으)세요		V-(으)세요
일어나다	일어나세요	운동하다	
만나다		전화하다	
읽다		공부하다	

▶ Look at the following picture and read it.

	커피 한 잔		물 _____ 병
	가방 _____ 개		친구 _____

■ 실력 다지기 Practice4

▶ Practice the following as in | ex |.

| ex |
콜라 하나 / 주다 → 콜라 하나 주세요.

① 여기 / 보다 → _____

② 이 책 / 사다 → _____

③ 이거 두 개 / 주다 → _____

④ 잠깐만 / 기다리다 → _____

단어 Vocabulary

일어나다 wake up   운동하다 exercise   공부하다 study   콜라 coke
사다 buy   잠깐만 for a minute   기다리다 wait

 있는 대화

☀ 피터가 카페에 갔습니다.

피터   여기요.① 커피 한 잔 주세요. 얼마예요?

직원   네.② 5,000원입니다.

피터   여기 있어요③.

직원   감사합니다. 잠깐만 기다리세요.

단어 Vocabulary

커피 coffee
얼마 how much
여기 here
잠깐만 for a minute
기다리다 wait
카페 cafe

💬 Choose the same thing as in the dialog.

① 여기는 (카페 / 커피)예요/이에요.

② 커피는 (오만 원 / 오천 원)이에요.

☀ Peter went to a cafe.

Peter   Excuse me. A cup of coffee, please. How much is it?

Staff   Well. It is 5,000 won.

Peter   Here you are.

Staff   Thank you. Wait a minute, please.

 맛있는 대화 TIP

① When calling a staff member at a restaurant, say "여기요" or "저기요". These days, there are many unmanned cafes as well as unmanned stores in Korea, and customers go to the counter to order directly even in the manned stores. But if you want to ask or request something to the staff, just say "여기요, 저기요".

② When answering, if positive, say "네". If it is negative, say "아니요".

③ Pronunciation: 있어요[이써요]

맛있는 연습 문제

1 How much is it? Try reading it.

①

가 얼마예요?

나 _____입니다.

50,000원

②

가 얼마예요?

나 _____이에요.

1,200원

③

가 얼마예요?

나 _____입니다.

16,000원

④

가 얼마예요?

나 _____.

23,000원

2 Listen carefully and complete the sentences.

Track 06-08

① _____.

② _____?

③ _____입니다.

④ 잠깐만 _____.

Korean Money

The currency unit of Korea is 'won'. There are coins and banknotes among Korean money.

 오백 원

 천 원

On the front side of Korean money, there are usually figures revered by the Korean people like King Sejong the Great and Admiral Yi Sunsin, and on the reverse side there are places or objects related to those figures.

세 종 대 왕

 백 원

 만 원

In Korea, many people prefer to pay by using a credit or debit card or through an app rather than by using cash such as coins or banknotes, and there are many ways to pay like that. In particular, these days, kiosks and unmanned cafes are rapidly increasing, so credit cards are used more than cash.

DAY 07

소유 말하기 Speaking about possession

- -

교통 카드가 있어요?

Do you have a transportation card?

지난 학습 **다시 보기 Review**

◆ **5,000원입니다.**

It is 5,000 won.

> '입니다' comes right after a noun to predicate its attribute or the class. 'N입니다' is used more officially or formally than 'N이에요/예요'.

- -

◆ **커피 한 잔 주세요.**

A cup of coffee, please.

> '–(으)세요' is used with a verb to request or command for an action of the verb politely.

• Look at the following and answer O if it is correct or X if it is incorrect.

① 선생님입니다.   (   )

② 물 둘 병 주세요.   (   )

③ 커피 셋 잔 주세요.   (   )

Point

학습 포인트

☆ Learn to express what you own.

☆ Learn to describe a fact or ask a question.

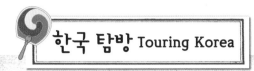
Heyri Art Valley, the largest art village in Korea, was founded in 1997 by many artists after they gathered in Paju, Gyeonggi-do.

Various galleries, themed museums with unique topics, performance halls, small theaters, and pretty cafes are clustered here, making it a worthwhile place to visit. You can also enjoy various works of art while walking along the trail called "Maeumi Datgil" that connects the east to the west of the village.

In addition, there are also many buildings where you can receive an artistic feeling, so why not visit this artist village once?

Sentence
핵심 문장

05 **교통 카드가 있어요?**
Do you have a transportation card?

06 **어디에서 사요?**
Where do you buy it?

05 교통 카드가 있어요?

Do you have a transportation card?

✓ N이/가 있어요[없어요]

It is used to talk about whether you have a thing or a person, etc. and the opposite.

	N		이/가 있어요[없어요]
Batchim O	볼펜	ballpoint pen	볼펜이 있어요. I have a ballpoint pen. 볼펜이 없어요. I don't have a ballpoint pen.
Batchim X	카드	card	카드가 있어요. I have a card. 카드가 없어요. I don't have a card.

ex 가방이 있어요. I have a bag.

한국 친구가 없어요. I have no Korean friend.

저는 휴대 전화가 없어요. I don't have a cell phone.

When you say the number together, you can say it in 'N이/가 N개[잔, 병, 명] 있어요'.

ex 가방이 다섯 개 있어요. I have five bags.

사과가 두 개 있어요. I have two apples.

한국 친구가 세 명 있어요. I have three Korean friends.

🔹 **TIP** If you want to ask whether someone has it or not, you can raise your accent.
  ex 한국 친구가 있어요? (↗) Do you have a Korean friend?
  볼펜이 있어요? (↗) Do you have a ballpoint pen?

🔹 **TIP** In speaking, '이/가' is sometimes dropped from 'N이/가'.
  ex 볼펜 있어요. I have a ballpoint pen.

단어 Vocabulary

휴대 전화 cell phone　　　사과 apple

실력 다지기 Practice1

▶ Practice the following as in |ex|.

|ex| 가방 → 가방이 있어요. 가방이 없어요.

① 콜라 → _____

② 형 → _____

③ 카드 → _____

④ 휴지 → _____

실력 다지기 Practice2

▶ Practice the following as in |ex|.

|ex| 가방 / 2개 → 가방이 두 개 있어요.

① 한국 친구 / 3명 → _____

② 콜라 / 4병 → _____

③ 지우개 / 1개 → _____

④ 오빠 / 2명 → _____

단어 Vocabulary

형 elder/older brother(to a male)   휴지 toilet paper   지우개 eraser
오빠 elder/older brother(to a female)

06 어디에서 사요?

Where do you buy it?

✓ V–아요/어요

'–아요/어요' is attached to a verb-stem to describe a fact or ask a question.

	basic form	–아요/어요	
ㅏ, ㅗ	앉다 sit	앉다 + 아요	앉아요
The others	먹다 eat	먹다 + 어요	먹어요
하다	공부하다 study	공부하다	공부해요

ex 지금 청소해요. I'm cleaning now.

매일 빵 먹어요. I eat bread every day.

TIP 자다(sleep) → 자 + 아요 → 자요   보다(see) → 보 + 아요 → 봐요

기다리다(wait) → 기다리 + 어요 → 기다려요   마시다(drink) → 마시 + 어요 → 마셔요

It changes like in the way above. This is the most commonly used terminating form in speaking situations. For basic Korean verbs, see page 38.

TIP If you want to ask a question, you can say it by raising your accent at the end.

ex 지금 공부해요? (↗) Are you studying now?

지금 밥 먹어요? (↗) Are you eating now?

✓ N에서

'N에서' is often used in 'N에서 V–아요/어요', and '에서' comes right after a place noun to say where the verb's action is performed.

ex 집에서 밥 먹어요. I eat at home.

공원에서 운동해요. I exercise in the park.

도서관에서 공부해요. I study in the library.

단어 Vocabulary

지금 now   매일 everyday   빵 bread   밥 meal

집 house, home   공원 park   운동하다 exercise   도서관 library

실력 다지기 Practice3

▶ Change the following words and fill in the blank.

	V–아요/어요
기다리다	기다려요
마시다	
책 읽다	
일어나다	
세수하다	
운동하다	

실력 다지기 Practice4

▶ Practice the following as in |ex|.

| |ex| 도서관 / 공부하다 → 저는 지금 도서관에서 공부해요. |

① 방 / 숙제하다 → 저는 지금 _____

② 회사 / 일하다 → 저는 지금 _____

③ 집 / 밥 먹다 → 저는 _____

④ 공원 / 친구 만나다 → _____

단어 Vocabulary

세수하다 wash up 　　방 room 　　숙제하다 do one's homework 　　회사 company
일하다 work

 있는 대화

☀ 안나와 피터가 교통 카드에 대해 이야기합니다.

안나   피터 씨, 교통 카드 있어요?

피터   네. 있어요.

안나   저는 교통 카드가 없어요①. 어디에서 사요?

피터   편의점②에서 사세요.

안나   아, 편의점에 있어요? 고마워요.

단어 Vocabulary

교통 카드 transportation card
어디 where
사다 buy
편의점 convenience store

💬 Summarize the dialog.

① 피터 씨는 _____이/가 있어요.

② 교통 카드는 _____에 있어요.

☀ Anna and Peter are talking about a transportation card.

Anna   Mr. Peter, do you have a transportation card?

Peter   Yes. I have.

Anna   I don't have a transportation card. Where do you buy it?

Peter   Buy it at a convenience store.

Anna   Oh, is it at a convenience store? Thank you.

 맛있는 대화 **TIP**

① Pronunciation: 없어요[업써요]

② Convenience stores in Korea sell various items. They also sell first-aid kits such as headache pills and digestive medicines. There is also a convenience store, at Hangang Park in Seoul, where you can directly cook your own ramen. Those who come to the Park for a walk or riding a bicycle stop by a convenience store to cook their own ramen. The taste of the ramen has delicacy.

맛있는 연습 문제

1 What do you have? Look at the pictures and make sentences.

① 안경이 _____.

② 휴대 전화가 _____.

③ _____ 있어요.

④ _____ 있어요.

⑤ _____ 있어요.

⑥ 여권이 _____.

Track 07-08

2 Listen carefully and complete the sentences.

① 교실에 _____ 있어요.

② 지금 _____ 밥 먹어요.

③ 매일 _____.

④ _____ 사요?

💠 **TIP** Sometimes, '휴대 전화(cell phone)' is referred to as '휴대폰' or '핸드폰'.

*단어 Vocabulary 우산 umbrella   안경 glasses   휴대 전화 cell phone
여권 passport   교실 classroom

Convenient public transportation in Korea

Public transportation in Korea is very convenient. In the case of Seoul, if you have a bus card when using public transportation, you can get a transfer discount.

If you have a transportation card or a credit card with the transportation card function when changing from subway to bus or from bus to subway, you will receive a discount. Other regions, such as Busan and Daegu also implement the service of transfer discounts depending on the region.

Transportation cards are sold at vending machines of subway stations, and you must hold the card at the terminal when getting on or off the bus or subway. However, be aware that you must transfer within 30 minutes to receive the discount, and you cannot receive a discount on buses of the same route.

A rechargeable transportation card may have a picture of a character or a celebrity, or you can make a card with your own picture. So, you can buy a card according to your preference. A disposable transit card, not a rechargeable transit card, can be usually purchased at subway stations.

사진제공(주민호)-한국관광공사

설명하기 Explaining

요즘도 한국어를 배워요?
Are you still learning Korean these days?

지난 학습 다시 보기 Review

◆ **교통 카드가 있어요?** ⟶ ○ ⟶ 'N이/가 있다[없다]' is used to talk about whether you
Do you have a transportation card? have a thing or a person, etc. and the opposite.

- -

◆ **어디에서 사요?** ⟶ ○ ⟶ '—아요/어요' is attached to a verb-stem
Where do you buy it? to describe a fact or ask a question.

- Look at the following and answer O if it is correct or X if incorrect.

　① 가방이 있어요.　　　　(　　　)

　② 도서관에서 공부하요.　(　　　)

　③ 책이 없어요.　　　　　(　　　)

Point

학습 포인트

☆ Learn the postposition to say a place.

☆ Learn the postposition to add another thing to something existing.

☆ Learn the postposition for the objective noun.

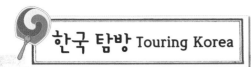

If you go by bus for about three hours from Seoul, you can see the East Sea. It is the Sea of clear and clean in Korea. Also is beautiful the coastal road developed along the Sea.

In particular, in Sokcho, Gangwon-do, there is Seoraksan Mountain, where you can hike, and there are many beaches nearby, so you can swim in the sea.

Sokcho Oeongchi Port Badahyanggiro is a beautiful place to take a walk while looking at the sea, and you can walk for about an hour along the Dulle-gil. They even filmed a drama here, so if you go to Sokcho, please go there once.

Sentence
핵심 문장

07 학교에 가요.
I go to school.

08 요즘도 한국어를 배워요?
Are you still learning Korean these days?

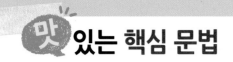

07 학교에 가요.

I go to school.

✓ N에

Place noun+에 가다(go)/오다(come) ▶ 'N에 가다/오다/있다/없다' is often used. '에' is mainly used to say what kind of action happens in the place(noun) just before itself.

 학교에 가요. I go to school.

휴대 전화가 집에 있어요. I have my cell phone at home.

Time noun+에 ▶ Also, it can be used with a time noun to say when an action is occurring. But, you don't need '에' in the case of '지금(now), 어제(yesterday), 오늘(today), 내일(tomorrow)'.

 주말에 집에서 숙제해요. I do my homework at home on the weekend.

오후에 학교에 가요. I go to school in the afternoon.

일요일에 집에서 쉬어요. I rest at home on Sunday.

🔅 **TIP** When you say a day of the week in Korean

주말 weekend

월요일	화요일	수요일	목요일	금요일	토요일	일요일
Monday	Tuesday	Wednesday	Thursday	Friday	Saturday	Sunday

🔅 **TIP** When speaking of a date with the month, say the month '일월, 이월, 삼월, 사월' first and then say '일일(first), 이일(second), 삼일(third), 사일(fourth)'. In cases of June and October, you should say '유월' for June and '시월' for October even though you should write '6월' and '10월'.

일월	이월	삼월	사월	오월	유월
January	February	March	April	May	June
칠월	팔월	구월	시월	십일월	십이월
July	August	September	October	November	December

 Vocabulary

학교 school   오후 afternoon   쉬다 take a rest

Track 08-02

실력 다지기 Practice1

▶ Look at the following sentences and choose the correct one.

① 집(에 / 에서) 가방이 있어요.

② 학교(에 / 에서) 한국 친구가 있어요.

③ 도서관(에 / 에서) 공부해요.

④ 노래방(에 / 에서) 노래해요.

⑤ 오늘 백화점(에 / 에서) 가요.

Track 08-03

실력 다지기 Practice2

▶ Listen carefully and complete the sentences.

① 월요일에 _____ 가요.

② _____ 파티가 있어요.

③ 9월 23일에 _____.

④ 주말에 _____.

단어 Vocabulary

노래방 karaoke   노래하다 sing   백화점 department store   파티 party

08 요즘도 한국어를 배워요?

Are you still learning Korean these days?

✓ N도

The postposition '도' comes right after a noun to say something that already exists or to include something else.

ex 저는 학생이에요. 제 동생도 학생이에요. I am a student. My younger brother is also a student.

가방에 책이 있어요. 공책도 있어요. There is a book in the bag. There is a notebook in it, too.

집에 우유가 없어요. 주스도 없어요. I don't have milk at home. No juice either.

✓ N을/를

The postposition '을/를' comes right after a noun an action directly affects. It's sometimes omitted when speaking.

	N		을/를
Batchim O	가방	bag	가방을
Batchim X	친구	friend	친구를

ex 동생은 밥을 먹어요. My younger brother eats rice.

민영 씨는 지금 빵을 사요. Minyoung is buying bread now.

제 친구는 한국어를 배워요. My friend is learning Korean.

내일 시험을 봐요. I have an exam tomorrow.

 Vocabulary

공책 notebook	우유 milk	주스 juice	배우다 learn
내일 tomorrow	시험 exam		

실력 다지기 Practice3

▶ Practice the following as in |ex|.

|ex| **친구 / 만나다 → 오늘 친구를 만나요.**

① 시험 / 보다   → 오늘 _____

② 컴퓨터 / 배우다   → _____

③ 책 / 읽다   → _____

실력 다지기 Practice4

▶ Use 'N도' to complete the conversation as in |ex|.

|ex| 가 **저는 피자를 좋아해요.**

나 **그래요? 저도 피자를 좋아해요.** (저 / 피자 / 좋아하다)

① 가 이 책은 윤기 씨 책이에요?

나 네. 윤기 씨 책이에요. _____ 윤기 씨 책이에요. (저 책)

② 가 집에 사과가 있어요?

나 네. 있어요. _____ 있어요. (바나나)

③ 가 여기요, 비빔밥 주세요. 그리고 _____ 주세요. (콜라)

나 네. 여기 있어요.

단어 Vocabulary

컴퓨터 computer   피자 pizza   좋아하다 like   그래요? Really?
그리고 and

맛있는 대화

☀ 민영과 또안이 바닷가에서 산책합니다.

민영　　또안 씨, 요즘도 한국어를 배워요?

또안　　네. 저는 매일 학교에① 가요.

민영　　그래요? 매일 수업이 있어요?

또안　　아니요. 하지만 매일 도서관에서 공부해요.

민영　　그래요? 저도 내일 도서관에 가요. 시험이 있어요.

　　　　우리 내일 학교에 같이② 가요. ③

단어 Vocabulary

요즘 these days
한국어 Korean (language)
매일 everyday
수업 class
아니다 no
하지만 but
도서관 library
공부하다 study
시험 exam
우리 we
같이 together

🗨 Choose the same thing as in the dialog.

① 또안은 요즘도 (한국어를 / 시험을) 공부해요.

② 민영은 (수업이 / 시험이) 있어요.

☀ Minyoung and Doan are taking a walk on the beach.

Minyoung	Mr. Doan, are you still learning Korean these days?
Doan	Yes. I go to school every day.
Minyoung	Do you? Do you have a class every day?
Doan	No. But I study in the library every day.
Minyoung	Do you? I'm going to the library tomorrow, too. I have a test. Let's go to school together.

 ## 맛있는 대화 TIP

① Pronunciation: 학교에[학꾜에]

② Pronunciation: 같이[가치]

③ When suggesting that we do something together, we often say it in the form of '같이 V−아요/어요' meaning 'Let's do ~ together'. It is raised slightly in the last part when speaking.

ex 같이 가요. (↗) Let's go together.

맛 있는 연습 문제

1 Listen carefully and complete the sentences.

① 내일 _____ 가요.

② _____ 시계가 있어요.

③ 매일 도서관에서 _____ 공부해요.

④ 우리 반에 중국 사람이 있어요. _____ 있어요.

2 Complete the conversation as in |ex|.

> |ex| 가 **민영 씨, 지금 뭐 해요?**
>
> 나 **도서관에서 책을 읽어요.** (도서관 / 책 / 읽다)

① 가 피터 씨, 지금 어디에 가요?

　 나 _____. (시장 / 가다)

② 가 또안 씨도 치킨을 좋아해요?

　 나 네. _____. (저 / 치킨 / 좋아하다)

③ 가 내일 파티에 가요?

　 나 네. _____? (또안 씨 / 파티 / 가다)

　 가 네. 저도 가요.

④ 가 내일 _____. (학교 앞 / 만나다)

　 나 네. 좋아요.

| *단어 Vocabulary | 시계 clock, watch | 반 class | 뭐 what | 시장 market |
| | 치킨 fried chicken | 앞 in front of | 좋다 good | |

Good place to study

Koreans go to the library a lot when they study. Because most schools have a library, there are many cases in which students often use the library inside the school.

And each region has a library. There is a "children's library" made for children, and there is also a youth library.

There are many people who study or work in a coffee shop rather than in a library. There are many people who study freely with friends in coffee shops because the library is so quiet that it is difficult to study while talking with friends. Nowadays, there are also "study cafes" that take advantage of libraries and cafes, so there are many people who study there.

Are Koreans studying really hard?

DAY 09

서술하기 Describing

한복이 정말 많아요.

There are so many hanboks.

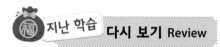

지난 학습 **다시 보기 Review**

◆ **학교에 가요.** ⟶ 'N에' is mainly used to say what kind of action takes place in the noun that indicates a place.

I go to school.

- -

◆ **요즘도 한국어를 배워요?** ⟶ '도' comes right after a noun to say something that already exists or to include something else.

Are you still learning Korean these days?

'을/를' comes right after a noun to say the object directly affected by an action.

• Look at the following and answer O if it is correct or X if incorrect.

① 또안 씨는 지금 노래방에 가요.　　(　　　)

② 피터 씨는 친구을 만나요.　　(　　　)

③ 민영 씨는 학교에 공부해요.　　(　　　)

Point

학습 포인트

☆ Learn expressions to say fact or ask a question.

☆ Learn about a phenomenon of '—' drop from a verb or an adjective.

If you go to Suwon, go to Hwaseong. Suwon Hwaseong is a fortress that was built by King Jeongjo, the 22nd king of the Joseon Dynasty, in memory of his father and it was a place to protect the country as well. You can see the science and architecture of the 18th century. By receiving the recognition of its beauty and value, it was designated as a UNESCO World Heritage Site in 1997.

There is also Suwon Hwaseong Haenggung, an annex of Suwon Hwaseong Fortress, which is the largest and most beautiful among Haenggung palaces. Haenggung is a place where the king stays outside the main palace, and various important events were held during the reign of King Jeongjo. Now, you are allowed to enter Suwon Hwaseong Haenggung for free if you wear hanbok according to the guidelines of KTO(Korea Tourism Organization).

Sentence
핵심 문장

09 한복이 정말 많아요.
There are so many hanboks.

10 정말 예뻐요.
It's really pretty.

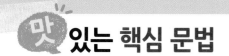 있는 핵심 문법

09

한복이 정말 많아요.

There are so many hanboks.

✓ N이/가 A-아요/어요

'-아요/어요' comes right after an adjective to describe a fact or ask a question.

	basic form		-아요/어요
ㅏ, ㅗ	좋다 good	좋다 + 아요	좋아요
The others	맛있다 delicious	맛있다 + 어요	맛있어요
하다	피곤하다 tired	피곤하다	피곤해요

Usually, it is often used in the form of 'N이/가 A-아요/어요'. There is no 'N을/를' in front of 'A-아요/어요'.

For basic Korean adjectives, see page 39.

ⓔⓧ 가방이 비싸요. The bag is expensive.

시계가 좋아요. The watch is good.

영화가 재미있어요. The movie is fun.

☀ **TIP** '좋다' is an adjective. That's why I say 'N이/가 좋아요'. '좋아하다' is a verb. That's why I say 'N을/를 좋아해요'.
　　ⓔⓧ 이 노래가 좋아요. This song is good.
　─　저는 이 노래를 좋아해요. I like this song.

단어 Vocabulary

비싸다 expensive　　　　재미있다 fun　　　　노래 song

실력 다지기 Practice1

▶ Change the following words and fill in the blank.

	A–아요/어요
싸다	싸요
비싸다	
맛있다	
맛없다	
재미없다	
따뜻하다	
시원하다	

실력 다지기 Practice2

▶ Practice the following as in |ex|.

| ex |
피자 / 맛있다 → 피자가 맛있어요.

① 친구 / 많다 → _____

② 날씨 / 맑다 → _____

③ 한국어 공부 / 재미있다 → _____

④ 비빔밥 / 좋다 → _____

단어 Vocabulary

싸다 cheap	맛없다 tasteless	재미없다 boring	따뜻하다 warm
시원하다 cool	많다 many	날씨 weather	맑다 clear

10

정말 예뻐요.

It's really pretty.

✓ '—' drop out

'—' is dropped in some adjective ending with '-아요/어요' or '-았어요/었어요', and is also dropped in some verb ending with it.

Adjectives	아프다 sick	아프다 + 아요	아파요
	바쁘다 busy	바쁘다 + 아요	바빠요
	나쁘다 bad	나쁘다 + 아요	나빠요
	배(가) 고프다 be hungry	배(가) 고프다 + 아요	배(가) 고파요
	예쁘다 pretty	예쁘다 + 어요	예뻐요
Verbs	쓰다 wear, write	쓰다 + 어요	써요
	끄다 turn off	끄다 + 어요	꺼요

ex 지금 배가 아파요. My stomach hurts right now.

오늘 바빠요. I'm busy today.

제 동생은 정말 예뻐요. My younger brother/sister is really cute/pretty.

모자를 써요. I wear a hat.

단어 Vocabulary

배 stomach, ship   정말 really, so   모자 hat

Track 09-05

실력 다지기 Practice3

▶ Change the following words and fill in the blank.

	–아요/어요
예쁘다	예뻐요
바쁘다	
배가 고프다	
날씨가 나쁘다	
편지를 쓰다	
불을 끄다	

실력 다지기 Practice4

Track 09-06

▶ Practice the following as in |ex|.

| ex | 배 / 고프다 → 배가 고파요.

① 머리 / 아프다 → _____

② 가방 / 예쁘다 → _____

③ 기분 / 나쁘다 → _____

④ 모자 / 쓰다 → _____

단어 Vocabulary

편지 letter   불 fire, light   머리 head   기분 feeling

 있는 대화

☀ 민영과 안나가 한복 가게에 갔습니다.

민영   여기가 한복 가게예요.

안나   한복이① 이렇게 많아요?

민영   네. 어느 한복이 마음에 들어요?②

안나   저 한복이 좋아요. 정말 예뻐요.

민영   네. 여기요. 이 한복 얼마예요?

단어 Vocabulary

한복 hanbok
가게 store
이렇게 like this
많다 many
어느 which
마음에 들다 like
정말 really, so

💬 Choose the same thing as in the dialog.

① 여기는 (학교 / 한복 가게)예요.

② 한복이 (예뻐요 / 없어요).

☀ Minyoung and Anna went to a hanbok store.

Minyoung	This is a hanbok store.
Anna	There are so many hanboks like this?
Minyoung	Yes. Which hanbok do you like?
Anna	I like that hanbok. It's really pretty.
Minyoung	Yes. Excuse me. How much is this hanbok?

 맛있는 대화 TIP

① Pronunciation: 한복이[한보기]

② When you think of a thing, object, location, or person as a good one, say 'N이/가 마음에 들어
요'.

ex 그 가방이 마음에 들어요. I like that bag.

여기가 마음에 들어요. I like here.

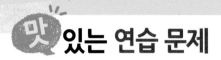
맛있는 연습 문제

1 Listen carefully and complete the sentences.

① 한복이 _____.

② 시계가 _____.

③ 날씨가 _____.

④ 다리가 _____.

2 Complete the conversation as in |ex|.

> |ex| 가 이 가방이 비싸요?
>
> 나 아니요. 싸요. (싸다)

① 가 날씨가 좋아요?

나 아니요. _____. (나쁘다)

② 가 불고기가 _____? (맛있다)

나 네. 그래서 불고기를 자주 먹어요.

③ 가 지금 뭐 해요?

나 영화를 봐요. 영화가 _____. (재미있다)

④ 가 어디 _____? (아프다)

나 아니에요. 괜찮아요.

*단어 Vocabulary | 다리 leg, bridge | 아니다 no | 불고기 bulgogi | 그래서 so
자주 often | 괜찮다 fine, ok

Korean traditional clothes, hanbok

The traditional clothes of Korea are Hanbok.
Koreans wear hanbok on holidays such as Lunar New Year's Day and Chuseok to greet their senior adults.

If you wear a hanbok and go to a palace like Gyeongbokgung Palace, you can enter for free. Recently, you can see a lot of young people wearing hanbok and taking pictures at the palace. There are also many shops that rent hanbok near the palace. Try on a beautiful hanbok and go to the palace to take a special photo.

Although hanbok is beautiful, it can be uncomfortable to wear on a regular basis. Therefore, there are many new designs of hanbok that can be worn on a daily basis, and the number of people who wear such daily hanbok is increasing.

이번 주 학습 내용 **Lessons This Week** -

DAY 06

◆ **N입니다** ▶ '입니다' comes right after a noun to predicate its attribute or the class. 'N입니다' is used more officially or formally than 'N이에요/예요'.

ⓔ저는 김민영입니다. 대학생입니다. I am Kim Minyoung. I am a college student.

피터 씨는 미국 사람입니다. Peter is an American.

◆ **V-(으)세요** ▶ '-(으)세요' is used with a verb to request or command for an action of the verb politely.

ⓔ나중에 전화하세요. Call me later, please.

비빔밥 하나 주세요. One bibimbap, please.

DAY 07

◆ **N이/가 있어요[없어요]** ▶ It is used to talk about whether(N이/가 있어요) or not(N이/가 없어요) you have a thing or person, etc.

ⓔ가방이 있어요. I have a bag.

한국 친구가 없어요. I have no Korean friend.

◆ **V-아요/어요** ▶ '-아요/어요' is attached to a verb-stem to describe a fact or ask a question.

ⓔ지금 청소해요. I'm cleaning now.

매일 빵 먹어요. I eat bread every day.

◆ **N에서** ▶ It is often used in 'N에서 V-아요/어요', and '에서' comes right after a place noun to say where the verb's action is performed.

ⓔ집에서 밥 먹어요. I eat at home.

공원에서 운동해요. I exercise in the park.

파이팅!

1 Connect the following words to form a sentence.

① 제 친구 / 한국 사람 ▷ _____

② 커피 / 한 잔 / 주다 ▷ _____

③ 지금 / 노트북 / 없다 ▷ _____

④ 저 / 노래방 / 노래하다 ▷ _____

[2-4] Listen carefully and choose the correct answer to the question.

Track 10-01

2 ① 내일 가요.
② 카드 주세요.
③ 16,500원입니다.

3 ① 네. 책이에요.
② 아니요. 없어요.
③ 네. 한국어를 공부해요.

4 ① 회사에서 일해요.
② 비빔밥 둘 주세요.
③ 시계가 한 개 있어요.

Track 10-02

5 Where is here? Listen carefully and choose the correct one.

① 가 식당　　　나 도서관　　　다 학교

② 가 노래방　　　나 백화점　　　다 우체국

*단어 Vocabulary　노트북 laptop　식당 restaurant　우체국 post office

DAY 08

◆ **N에** ▶ It is often used as 'N(place noun)에 가다, 오다, 있다, 없다'. '에' comes right after a place noun to say what kind of action takes place in the place.

  ⓔⓧ 학교에 가요. I go to school.

     휴대 전화가 집에 있어요. I have my cell phone at home.

◆ **N도** ▶ '도' comes right after a noun to say the addition or inclusion of another thing to something already existing.

  ⓔⓧ 저는 학생이에요. 제 동생도 학생이에요. I am a student. My younger brother is also a student.

     가방에 책이 있어요. 공책도 있어요. There is a book in the bag. There is a notebook in it, too.

◆ **N을/를** ▶ '을/를' is a postposition that comes right after a noun an action directly affects.

  ⓔⓧ 동생은 밥을 먹어요. My younger brother eats rice.

     제 친구는 한국어를 배워요. My friend is learning Korean.

DAY 09

◆ **N이/가 A−아요/어요** ▶ '−아요/어요' comes right after an adjective to describe a fact or ask a question. 'N을/를' does not come before 'A−아요/어요'.

  ⓔⓧ 가방이 비싸요. The bag is expensive.

     영화가 재미있어요. The movie is fun.

◆ **'ㅡ' drop out** ▶ When '−아/어−' comes at the end of some adjective, '아프다(sick), 바쁘다(busy), 예쁘다 (pretty), etc.', and verbs like '쓰다(write), 끄다(turn off), etc.', 'ㅡ' is dropped.

  ⓔⓧ 지금 배가 아파요. My stomach hurts right now.

     가방이 예뻐요. The bag is beautiful.

◀ 실력 다지기 Practice2 ▶

1 Connect the following words to form a sentence.

① 윤기 씨 / 공원 / 가다 ▷ _____

② 안나 씨 / 태권도 / 배우다 ▷ _____

③ 또안 씨 / 오늘 / 바쁘다 ▷ _____

④ 제 고양이 / 예쁘다 ▷ _____

[2-4] Listen carefully and choose the correct answer to the question.

2 ① 네. 있어요.

② 집에 있어요.

③ 네. 책이에요.

3 ① 고마워요.

② 네. 아파요.

③ 네. 밥을 먹어요.

4 ① 네. 재미없어요.

② 네. 재미있어요.

③ 아니요. 재미있어요.

5 Listen carefully and choose the same thing as in the conversation.

① 남자는 병원에 가요.

② 남자는 병원에서 일해요.

③ 남자는 지금 병원에 있어요.

*단어 Vocabulary   태권도 Taekwondo   고양이 cat   남자 man   병원 hospital

📷 Shall we go to the central region of Korea?

There are many places in Gyeonggi-do that used to be filming sites for dramas. Anseong Mirinae Fortress Site, Hantangang Sky Bridge in Pocheon, and Hyowon Park in Suwon are those places. In addition, there are Outlets in Paju and Yeoju where you can do the shopping, and Art Valley in Pocheon has plenty of things to see. And there are many places like Yangpyeong and Gapyeong where you can see the beauty of nature.

Mirinae Fortress Site

Hantangang Sky Bridge

Art Valley

You can feel the beautiful and cozy atmosphere in many sites in Korea like this.

Korea has four distinct seasons, spring, summer, autumn, and winter. Because the attraction to be felt every season is different, it is beautiful whenever people come. The flowers bloom in spring and the leaves turn red in autumn, so there are many people who visit the mountain in spring and autumn. During the hot summer months, there are usually many people on vacation. Some go on vacation to a beach with a wide and cool sea. Being cold it snows often and is beautiful in its winter. There are many people who visit Gangwon-do to enjoy skiing and snowboarding, which are representative winter sports. As there are many mountains and seas in the province, you can feel the beauty of Korea there anytime in spring, summer, autumn, or winter. Also is famous the city Pyeongchang in the province, for the 2018 Pyeongchang Winter Olympics was held there, and there is also Hongcheon at which beef is famous.

맛으로
만나 보는
한국
Korea through taste

Wondering what food you must try when you visit Gangwon-do? Since there are many potatoes in Gangwon-do, people have eaten a lot of food made with potatoes since olden times. And there are also a lot of corns there. However, it is relatively spacious, so there is a difference in its famous foods in each part of its area.

🏅 닭갈비 Dakgalbi(Spicy stir-fried chicken)

If you go to Chuncheon, Gangwon-do, you must try the dakgalbi. Dakgalbis are a little bit spicy but delicious. You can try dakgalbi in Seoul, but the dakgalbi in Chuncheon tastes better. It's also a good idea to try cold makguksu with dakgalbi.

🏅 생선회 Saengseonhoe(Sashimi)

Gangwon-do is near the clean sea, so you can enjoy saengseonhoe. The saengseonhoe in Gangwon-do is fresh and the price is relatively cheap, so lots of people come to eat it. If you travel near the sea, you can eat it anywhere near the East Sea, the South Sea, or the West Sea. But the menu is slightly different according to the region because the fish caught differs in each region. If you are traveling near the sea, it is a good idea for you to try the fresh saengseonhoe.

이렇게 말해요! **Say like this!**

When ordering dakgalbi, you say "인분", but again, you can only say the number without using the unit noun.

닭갈비 이 인분 주세요. = 닭갈비 둘 주세요.

Dakgalbi for two persons, please.　　　　Two dakgalbis, please.

WEEK 03

DAY 11-15

한국의 문화 도시로 떠나 볼까요?

Shall we go to the **cultural city** of Korea?

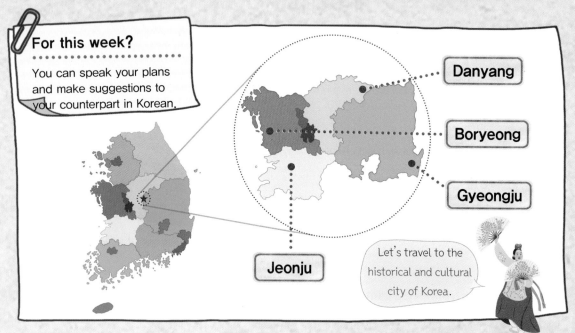

For this week?

You can speak your plans and make suggestions to your counterpart in Korean.

Danyang

Boryeong

Gyeongju

Jeonju

Let's travel to the historical and cultural city of Korea.

DAY 11

계획 말하기

Speaking about plans

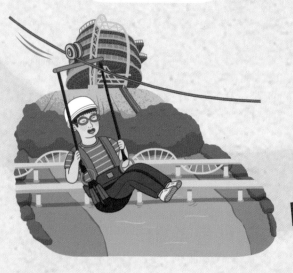

DAY 12

과거와 희망 말하기

Speaking about the past and hope

DAY 13 수단 표현하기
Expressing the means

DAY 14 제안하기
Making a suggestion

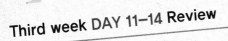

DAY 15

Third week DAY 11–14 Review

Review the main lessons of DAY 11–14, and check your Korean with various questions.

Travel & Culture in Korea

What kind of historical and cultural cities are there in Korea? Let's take a look together.

DAY 11

계획 말하기 Speaking about plans

친구들하고 파티를 할 거예요.

I will have a party with my friends.

지난 학습 **다시 보기 Review**

◆ **한복이 정말 많아요.**

There are so many hanboks.

> '-아요/어요' comes right after an adjective to describe a fact or ask a question.

◆ **정말 예뻐요.**

It's really pretty.

> '—' is dropped in some adjective ending with '-아요/어요' or '-았어요/었어요', and is also dropped in some verb ending with it.

• Look at the following and answer O if it is correct or X if it is incorrect.

① 가방이가 비싸요.　　(　　)

② 윤기 씨는 요즘 바빠요.　(　　)

③ 날씨가 따뜻하요.　　(　　)

학습 포인트 Point

☆ Learn expressions for future plans.

☆ Learn expressions to describe something you do together.

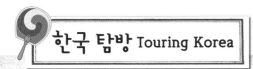

Danyang, Chungcheongbuk-do is a quiet and beautiful place. The place named 'Eight Scenic Views of Danyang' is famous for their magnificent sceneries.

You can also enjoy the panoramic view of Danyang, looking down to the scenery from the 'Mancheonha Skywalk'.

At the Danyang Glide Factory, there are various activities that you could try out, such as zip-wire, hang gliding and paragliding. There are five gliding sites and practice fields, open all levels from beginner to experienced glider. It is located at the top of Yangbangsan Mountain.

11 이번 주말에 뭐 할 거예요?

What will you do this weekend?

12 친구들하고 파티를 할 거예요.

I will have a party with my friends.

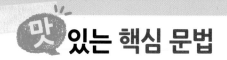

11 이번 주말에 뭐 할 거예요?

What will you do this weekend?

✓ V-(으)ㄹ 거예요

'-(으)ㄹ 거예요' comes grammarticaly right after a verb to describe the future plans. Usually the grammar is applied to Korean verbs, for example '가다(go), 먹다(eat), 공부하다(study), 청소하다(cleaning)', etc.

	basic form	-(으)ㄹ 거예요
Batchim O	먹다 eat	먹을 거예요 will eat
Batchim X	오다 come	올 거예요 will come

ex 저는 이따 커피를 마실 거예요. I will have a coffee later.

내일 책을 읽을 거예요. I will read a book tomorrow.

가 내일 뭐 할 거예요? What are you going to do tomorrow?

나 숙제할 거예요. I will do my homework.

가 토요일에 어디에 갈 거예요? Where are you going to go on Saturday?

나 박물관에 갈 거예요. I'm going to go to the museum.

TIP An adjectives such as '예쁘다(pretty), 바쁘다(busy), 좋다(good)' cannot be used with '-(으)ㄹ 거예요' which is to discuss about a plan. If this grammar is used with adjectives, instead of 'V-(으)ㄹ 거예요?', it will be 'A-(으)ㄹ 거예요?', and it's referring to guessing, not planning.

TIP Pronunciation: 먹을 거예요[머글꺼예요], 올 거예요[올꺼예요]

단어 Vocabulary

이따 later   토요일 Saturday   박물관 museum

Grammar

실력 다지기 Practice1

▶ Change the following words and fill in the blank.

	V-(으)ㄹ 거예요
회사에 가다	회사에 갈 거예요
친구를 만나다	
한국어를 공부하다	
밥을 먹다	
옷을 입다	

실력 다지기 Practice2

▶ Select the most suitable word from ┃ex┃ to complete the conversation.

┃ex┃ 읽다   쉬다   여행하다   쇼핑하다

① 가 주말에 뭐 할 거예요?

  나 백화점에서 _____.

② 가 내일 뭐 해요?

  나 집에서 _____.

③ 가 저녁에 뭐 해요?

  나 책을 _____.

④ 가 방학에 뭐 할 거예요?

  나 제주도에서 _____.

단어 Vocabulary

옷 clothes   입다 wear   여행하다 travel   쇼핑하다 go shopping
저녁 evening   방학 vacation   제주도 Jejudo Island

12 친구들하고 파티를 할 거예요.

I will have a party with my friends.

✓ N하고

'하고' comes right after a personage-noun to describe that the person is grouped with someone/something together.

- 민영 씨는 친구하고 도서관에서 공부해요. Minyoung is studying with her friend in the library.

  윤기 씨하고 같이 가세요. Go with Yoonki.

  저는 방학에 또안 씨하고 피터 씨하고 제주도에 갈 거예요.

  I'm going to Jejudo Island with Doan and Peter for vacation.

By writing the form of 'N하고 N', you can connect each of the nouns as having the equivalent qualification.

- 또안 씨는 빵하고 우유를 먹어요. Doan is eating bread with milk.

  저는 백화점에서 구두하고 모자를 살 거예요.

  I will buy a pair of shoes and a hat at the department store.

> **TIP** 'N(이)랑', 'N와/과' and 'N하고' have the same meaning. 'N하고' and 'N(이)랑' are mainly used when talking.
> - 가 주말에 뭐 할 거예요? What will you do on the weekend?
>   나 주말에 친구랑 영화를 볼 거예요. I will watch a movie with my friend on the weekend.
>
>   가 누구하고 밥을 먹어요? Who will you eat with?
>   나 친구랑 먹어요. I will eat with my friend.

 단어 Vocabulary

구두 shoes

실력 다지기 Practice3

▶ Look at the following picture and read it.

		하고
커피	빵	커피하고 빵
책	볼펜	
휴대 전화	교통 카드	
밥	라면	

실력 다지기 Practice4

▶ Practice the following as in |ex|.

|ex|
> **친구 / 밥 / 먹다** → 안나 씨는 친구하고 밥을 먹어요.

① 민영 씨 / 같이 / 도서관 / 가다 → 저는 오늘 _____.

② 콜라 / 우유 / 사다 → 윤기 씨는 편의점에서 _____.

③ 동생 / 백화점 / 쇼핑하다 → 저는 내일 _____.

④ 사과 / 피자 / 좋아하다 → 저는 _____.

단어 Vocabulary

라면 ramen

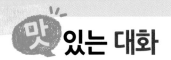 있는 대화

☀️ 또안과 윤기가 치킨을 먹으면서 이야기합니다.

또안	치킨이 진짜 맛있어요.
	그런데 이번 주말에 뭐① 할 거예요?

윤기	저는 친구하고 같이 단양에 여행 갈 거예요.
	또안 씨는 뭐 할 거예요?

또안	저는 친구들하고 같이 파티를 할 거예요.

윤기	그래요? 어디에서 해요?

또안	우리② 집에서 할 거예요.

단어 Vocabulary

진짜 really, so
그런데 by the way, but
이번 this time
주말 weekend
뭐 what
여행 trip
들 -s[plural]
파티 party
집 house, home

💬 Summarize the dialog.

① 또안 씨는 주말에 _____.

② 파티는 _____에서 할 거예요.

☀ Doan and Yoonki are chatting while they are having the fried chicken.

Doan   The fried chicken is really delicious.

        But what will you do this weekend?

Yoonki   I will go on a trip to Danyang with my friend.

        What will you do, Mr. Doan?

Doan   I will have a party with my friends.

Yoonki   Are you? Where are you doing it?

Doan   We will do it at home.

 맛있는 대화 **TIP**

① '뭐' refers to a fact or thing that you do not know. And by writing '을/를' with '뭐', it can be said '뭐를'. In this case, '뭐를' can be shortened to '뭘'.

   ex 뭐를 먹어요? = 뭘 먹어요? What are you eating?

② Korea has a culture that appreciate 'us/we' more. Instead of using '제 집(my house), 제 학교(my school)', we often use '우리 집(our house), 우리 학교(our school)'.

맛있는 연습 문제

1 Look at the picture and complete the conversation as in |ex|.

| ex |

가 **내일 뭐 할 거예요?**

나 **공부할 거예요.**

①

가 주말에 뭐 할 거예요?

나 _____.

②

가 저녁에 뭐 할 거예요?

나 _____.

③

가 오후에 뭐 할 거예요?

나 _____.

④

가 금요일에 뭐 할 거예요?

나 _____.

Track 11-08

2 Listen carefully and complete the sentences.

① 내일 _____.

② _____ 사요.

③ _____ 같이 명동에 _____.

*단어 Vocabulary 명동 Myeong-dong

116

KOREA

What I usually do on weekend

What do you usually do on the weekend? Usually, on weekends, most of the people would rest at home. It is the same for most Koreans. But instead of resting at home, I go to the 'jjimjilbang' or sauna, otherwise to a 'PC Bang' or 'Multi Bang' to have fun with my friends.

Have you heard of jjimjilbang? As you take a rest, sweating due to the steam in a jjimjilbang, you can bet the fatigue of the week will be relieved. There, you can be served special foods or drinks, for example, hard-boiled eggs or sikhye (the traditional Korean sweet rice cooling tea). They are delicious and can be enjoyed by people of all ages.

People who love to sing can also choose to relieve their stress by singing their lungs out at the karaoke. Nowadays karaoke box is so popular. You can sing one to two songs by paying 500 won (~$0.40) only.

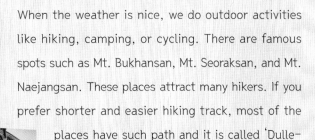

When the weather is nice, we do outdoor activities like hiking, camping, or cycling. There are famous spots such as Mt. Bukhansan, Mt. Seoraksan, and Mt. Naejangsan. These places attract many hikers. If you prefer shorter and easier hiking track, most of the places have such path and it is called 'Dulle-gil'.

지난 주말에 머드 축제에 갔어요.
I went to the Mud Festival last weekend.

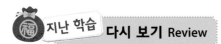

지난 학습 **다시 보기 Review**

◆ **이번 주말에 뭐 할 거예요?**
   What will you do this weekend?

> '-(으)ㄹ 거예요' is attached to a verb-stem to describe the future plans.

◆ **친구들하고 파티를 할 거예요.**
   I will have a party with my friends.

> '하고' comes right after a personage-noun to describe that the person is doing something together with or is being connected together as having the equivalent qualification.

◆ Look at the following and answer O if it is correct or X if incorrect.

   ① 주말에 집에서 공부할 거예요.   (   )

   ② 친구하고 밥을 먹어요.   (   )

   ③ 형하고 영화를 볼 거예요.   (   )

Point
학습 포인트

☆ Learn expressions of the past.

☆ Learn to express hope.

There are lots of attractive festivals happening in each region of Korea. The Mud Festival is held every July at Daecheon Beach in Boryeong, Chungcheongnam-do. This is one of the well-known festivals that attract visitors from all around the world.

You can learn more about mud at the Mud Experience Center or sign up for an experience program at the Mud Square Experience Booth. Not only that, you can also try out the mud self-massage zone, take mud rides and watch performances at the festival. It is highly recommended to try to take a bath at the beach too.

Sentence
핵심 문장

13 지난 주말에 머드 축제에 갔어요.
I went to the Mud Festival last weekend.

14 저도 가고 싶어요.
I want to go, too.

13 지난 주말에 머드 축제에 갔어요.

I went to the Mud Festival last weekend.

✓ V/A-았어요/었어요

'–았어요/었어요' is attached at the end of a verb or adjective to describe something happened in the past.

	basic form	–았어요/었어요	
ㅏ, ㅗ	앉다 sit	앉다 + 았어요	앉았어요 sat
The others	먹다 eat	먹다 + 었어요	먹었어요 ate
하다	공부하다 study	공부하다	공부했어요 studied

- ⓔⓧ 작년에 제주도에 여행 갔어요. I went on a trip to Jejudo Island last year.

  어제 영화를 봤어요. 아주 재미있었어요. I watched a movie yesterday. It was really interesting.

Right after a noun, use '이었어요/였어요'.

- ⓔⓧ 어제는 제 생일이었어요. It was my birthday yesterday.

  저는 기자였어요. I was a reporter.

> 🖊 **TIP** Raise the intonation at the end of a sentence if you wish to ask a question.
> ⓔⓧ 커피 마셨어요? (↗) Did you drink coffee?
> 숙제했어요? (↗) Did you do your homework?

단어 Vocabulary

작년 last year 　　　　아주 very, really 　　　　생일 birthday 　　　　기자 reporter

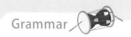

실력 다지기 Practice1

▶ Change the following words and fill in the blank.

	V-았어요/었어요
보다	봤어요
오다	
읽다	
만나다	
기다리다	
운동하다	

	A-았어요/었어요
좋다	좋았어요
비싸다	
맛있다	
재미없다	
따뜻하다	
시원하다	

실력 다지기 Practice2

▶ Practice the following as in |ex|.

| ex |

밥을 먹다 → 밥을 먹었어요.

① 주말에 백화점에 가다 → _____

② 그 영화가 재미있다 → _____

③ 어제 좀 피곤하다 → _____

④ 어제 집에서 청소하다 → _____

⑤ 친구하고 카페에서 숙제하다 → _____

단어 Vocabulary

좀 a little   피곤하다 tired

14

저도 가고 싶어요.

I want to go, too.

✓ V-고 싶다

'-고 싶다' comes at the end of a verb to say that you want something.

	basic form	-고 싶다
Batchim O	먹다 eat	먹고 싶다 want to eat
Batchim X	가다 go	가고 싶다 want to go

ex 제주도에 가고 싶어요. I want to go to Jejudo Island.

치킨을 먹고 싶어요. I want to have fried chicken.

한국어를 배우고 싶어요. I want to learn Korean language.

If what you want is a thing in the past, you can say '-고 싶었어요'.

ex 지난주에는 집에서 쉬고 싶었어요. Last week I wanted to rest at home.

언니, 정말 보고 싶었어요. Sister, I really missed you.

TIP Raise the last part when you ask what your counterpart wants.
ex 뭐 하고 싶어요? (↗) What do you want to do?

You can say '-고 싶어 하다' when talking about the hope of a third party rather than the one of your talking counterpart.

ex 가 주말에 뭐 할 거예요? What are you going to do on the weekend?

나 동생이 노래방에 가고 싶어 해요. 그래서 노래방에 갈 거예요.

My younger brother wants to go to karaoke. So, I'm going to go for karaoke.

 Vocabulary

지난주 last week   쉬다 take a rest

Track 12-05

실력 다지기 Practice3

▶ Change the following words and fill in the blank.

	V-고 싶어요
도서관에 가다	도서관에 가고 싶어요
밥을 먹다	
책을 읽다	
영화를 보다	
공원에서 산책하다	
집에서 운동하다	

실력 다지기 Practice4

Track 12-06

▶ Practice the following as in |ex|.

|ex| 한국어를 배우다 → 한국어를 배우고 싶어요.

① 콘서트에 가다 → _____

② 청바지를 사다 → _____

③ 그 노래를 듣다 → _____

④ 그 배우를 만나다 → _____

⑤ 케이크를 만들다 → _____

단어 Vocabulary

산책하다 take a walk   콘서트 concert   청바지 jeans   듣다 listen
케이크 cake   만들다 make

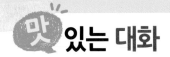 **있는 대화**

☀ 안나와 민영이 주말에 한 일에 대해 이야기합니다.

민영	주말에 뭐 했어요?

안나 토요일에 머드 축제에 갔어요.

정말^① 재미있었어요.

민영 그래요? 머드 축제는 어떻게 알았어요?

안나 인터넷에서 봤어요. 다음 주말에는 동강에 갈 거예요.

민영 씨도 같이 가요.

민영 네. 좋아요. 저도 가고 싶어요.

단어 Vocabulary

주말 weekend
머드 mud
축제 festival
어떻게 how
알다 know
인터넷 internet
다음 next
동강 Donggang River

 Summarize the dialog.

① 안나 씨는 지난 주말에 머드 축제에 _____.

② 안나 씨하고 민영 씨는 다음 주말에 동강에 _____.

☀ Anna and Minyoung are talking about what they did over the weekend.

Minyoung	What did you do over the weekend?
Anna	I went to a Mud Festival on Saturday. It was really fun.
Minyoung	Was it? How did you know about the Mud Festival?
Anna	I saw it on the internet. I'm going to Donggang River next weekend. Would you like to come along, Ms. Minyoung?
Minyoung	Yes. I like it. I want to go there too.

 맛있는 대화 **TIP**

① '너무(too)' and '정말(really)' placed before a verb or adjective have similar meaning. However, '정말' can be used to emphasize that the statement is 'real' and it can be used as in '정말이에요'. But '너무' cannot be used as in '너무예요'.

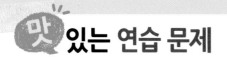있는 연습 문제

1 Complete the conversation as in |ex|.

> |ex| 가 어제 뭐 했어요?
>
> 나 친구하고 한강 공원에서 산책했어요. (산책하다)

① 가 그 영화 봤어요?

나 네. 정말 _____. (재미있다)

② 가 주말에 뭐 했어요?

나 집에서 _____. (쉬다)

③ 가 어제 뭐 했어요?

나 친구를 _____. (만나다)

2 Complete the conversation as in |ex|.

> |ex| 가 한국 노래를 듣고 싶어요. (듣다)
>
> 나 그래요? 그럼 이 노래 같이 들어요.

① 가 주말에 뭐 할 거예요?

나 한강 공원에서 자전거를 _____. (타다)

② 가 노래방에 _____. (가다)

나 그래요? 지금 같이 가요.

③ 가 백화점에 갈 거예요. 모자를 살 거예요.

나 저도 같이 가요. 구두를 하나 _____. (사다)

🔖 **TIP** '듣다(listen)' is an irregular verb that changes 'ㄷ' to 'ㄹ' when it encounters '-아/어-' or '-으-' as in '-아요/어요' or '-았어요/었어요'. So you have to say, '들어요' or '들었어요'.

*단어 Vocabulary 그럼 and, then 자전거 bike 타다 ride

Korea's regional specialties

What specialties are there in Korea? There are different regional specialty products by region. Lots of amusing festivals open under the theme of the specialty product. Icheon, famous for rice, has the Rice Festival, Ginseng Festival opens in Geumsan where ginseng is famous, Cheongsong, famous for apples, has the Apple Festival, and Paste Festival opens in Sunchang, famous for red pepper paste. There are also many amusing festivals in the Korean region, for example, the Sancheoneo Festival in Hwacheon, Gangwon-do, and the Chimaek Festival in Daegu. So it is a good idea to find out whether there is any festival before traveling to Korea.

KTX로 가세요.

Go by KTX.

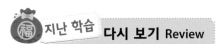
지난 학습 **다시 보기** Review

♦ **지난 주말에 머드 축제에 갔어요.**

I went to the Mud Festival last weekend.

> '−았어요/었어요' is attached at the end of a verb or adjective to describe something happened in the past.

♦ **저도 가고 싶어요.**

I want to go too.

> '−고 싶다' comes at the end of a verb to say that you want something.

● Look at the following and answer O if it is correct or X if incorrect.

① 윤기 씨는 카페에 갔어요.　　　(　　)

② 커피를 마셔고 싶어요.　　　(　　)

③ 어제 한국어를 공부했어요.　　　(　　)

Point
학습 포인트

☆ Learn how to use a postposition to say a means or method.

☆ Learn about the irregular change of a verb or an adjective in the 'ㅂ' Batchim.

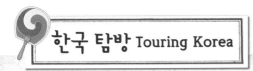

Are you interested in Korean history? If you want to see Korean history, go to Gyeongju. In Gyeongju, the entire city is a cultural heritage.

It is a place where you can see beautiful cultural heritages such as Cheomseongdae, the oldest observatory, Anapji Pond where the king of Silla held a feast, and Bulguksa Temple, a world heritage site, and Seokguram Grotto.

The tomb of King Munmu the Great is also worth a visit to Gyeongju. It is in the middle of the sea, and he is the King of the Silla Dynasty. He asked his people to sprinkle the remains of his corpse ash on the sea to protect his country even after he died.

Be sure to visit Gyeongju, the beautiful historical city.

Bulguksa Temple

Seokguram Grotto

Cheomseongdae

Sentence
핵심 문장

15 **KTX로 가세요.**
Go by KTX.

16 **경주는 정말 아름다워요.**
Gyeongju is really beautiful.

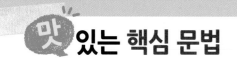

15

KTX로 가세요.

Go by KTX.

✓ N(으)로

It is used to express a means, method, tool or direction for doing something.

	N		(으)로
Batchim O	숟가락	spoon	숟가락으로 with spoon
Batchim X	카드	card	카드로 by card
'ㄹ' Batchim	독일	Germany	독일로 to Germany

> ☆ **TIP** After a noun with a 'ㄹ' Batchim, only '로' is used, not '으로'.
>
> ㉣ 한국 사람은 젓가락으로 밥을 먹어요. Koreans eat with chopsticks.
>
> 지금 길이 막혀요. 지하철로 가세요. The road is blocked now. Go by subway.

N(으)로 N 시간(분) 걸려요 ▶ It is used to express the duration or time needed for something.

㉣ 제 고향에서 한국까지 비행기로 두 시간 걸려요.

It takes two hours by flight from my hometown to South Korea.

회사까지 자전거로 30분 걸려요. It takes 30 minutes to get to work by bicycle.

'N(으)로' is not recommended to use together with '타다'.

㉣ 지하철로 타요. (X)   지하철로 가요. (O) I'm going by subway.

자전거로 타요. (X)   자전거로 가요. (O) I go by bicycle.

> ☆ **TIP** It can also be used to say direction.
>
> ㉣ 내일 제주도로 출발해요. I'm leaving for Jejudo Island tomorrow.
>
> 이쪽으로 오세요. This way please.
>
> 다음 주에 서울로 갈 거예요. I'm going to Seoul next week.

단어 Vocabulary

젓가락 chopsticks	길이 막히다 clogged	지하철 subway	시간 hour, time
분 minute	걸리다 take time	고향 hometown	비행기 flight
출발하다 depart, leave	이쪽 this way	다음 주 next week	서울 Seoul

실력 다지기 Practice1

▶ Look at the following sentences and choose the correct one.

① 휴대 전화(로 / 으로) 사진을 찍어요.

② 부산에 비행기(로 / 으로) 왔어요.

③ 지하철(로 / 으로) 갈 거예요.

④ 라면을 젓가락(로 / 으로) 먹어요.

실력 다지기 Practice2

▶ Practice the following as in | ex |.

| ex |
경주에 KTX로 가요. (KTX)

① 친구하고 제주도에 _____ 갈 거예요. (배)

② _____ 영화를 봐요. (휴대 전화)

③ _____ 말하세요. (한국말)

④ 여기까지 _____ 한 시간 걸렸어요. (택시)

단어 Vocabulary

사진 picture	찍다 take	부산 Busan	라면 ramen
경주 Gyeongju	말하다 speak	한국말 Korean	택시 taxi

16 경주는 정말 아름다워요.

Gyeongju is really beautiful.

✓ 'ㅂ' irregular

When an adjective-stem or verb-stem ends in 'ㅂ', the 'ㅂ' changes to '–오/우–' with an ending that starts in the vowel, '–아/어–' or '–았/었–'.

	–아요/어요	–았어요/었어요
덥다 hot	더워요 is hot	더웠어요 was hot
춥다 cold	추워요 is cold	추웠어요 was cold
쉽다 easy	쉬워요 is easy	쉬웠어요 was easy
어렵다 difficult	어려워요 is difficult	어려웠어요 was difficult
맵다 spicy	매워요 is spicy	매웠어요 was spicy
귀엽다 cute	귀여워요 is cute	귀여웠어요 was cute
무겁다 heavy	무거워요 is heavy	무거웠어요 was heavy
가볍다 light	가벼워요 is light	가벼웠어요 was light
돕다 help	도와요 help	도왔어요 helped

ex 오늘 좀 추워요. It's a little cold today.

시험이 어려웠어요. The exam was difficult.

제 동생은 정말 귀여워요. My younger brother is really cute.

가방이 무거워요. The bag is heavy.

윤기 씨는 친구를 잘 도와요. Yoonki is good at helping his friends.

단어 Vocabulary

좀 a little   잘 well

132

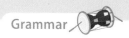

실력 다지기 Practice3

▶ Practice the following as in |ex|.

| ex | **날씨 / 덥다** → 날씨가 더워요.

① 떡볶이 / 맵다 → _____

② 시험 / 쉽다 → _____

③ 인형 / 귀엽다 → _____

④ 경치 / 아름답다 → _____

실력 다지기 Practice4

▶ Practice the following as in |ex|.

| ex | **날씨 / 덥다** → 날씨가 더웠어요.

① 날씨 / 춥다 → _____

② 음식 / 맵다 → _____

③ 제 동생 / 귀엽다 → _____

④ 가방 / 가볍다 → _____

단어 Vocabulary

떡볶이 tteokbokki   인형 doll   경치 scenery   아름답다 beautiful   음식 food

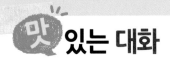 있는 대화

☀ 안나와 윤기가 텔레비전을 봅니다.

안나　윤기 씨, 저기가 경주예요? 정말 아름다워요.

윤기　맞아요. 경주는 정말 아름다워요.

안나　저도 가고 싶어요. 그런데 경주에 어떻게 가요?

윤기　KTX로 가세요. KTX가 빨라요①.

안나　서울에서 경주까지② 얼마나 걸려요?

윤기　KTX로 두 시간③쯤 걸려요.

단어 Vocabulary
맞다 That's right
빠르다 fast
얼마나 how long
걸리다 take time
시간 hour, time
쯤 about

💬 Summarize the dialog.

① 서울에서 경주까지 _____(으)로 _____ 걸려요.

② 경주는 _____.

☀ Anna and Yoonki are watching TV.

Anna   Mr. Yoonki, is that Gyeongju? It's really beautiful.

Yoonki   That's right. Gyeongju is really beautiful.

Anna   I would like to go, too. But how can I go there?

Yoonki   You can go by KTX. It's fast.

Anna   How long does it take from Seoul to Gyeongju?

Yoonki   It takes about two hours by KTX.

 맛있는 대화 TIP

① '빠르다' is irregular because when it is combined with '–아/어', another 'ㄹ' is formed and becomes 'ㄹㄹ'. So it becomes '빨라요'. The same pattern also happens in the case of '모르다 (do not know)'. So, '모르다' becomes '몰라요' by meeting '–아요'.

② 'N1에서 N2까지(from N1 to N2)' is used with place nouns to say the starting point and the ending point.

③ When talking about how long it takes, the unit is '분(minute)' as in '오 분(five minutes), 십 분 (ten minutes), 삼십 분(thirty minutes)'. The unit of time is not '일 시간, 이 시간', but '한 시간 (one hour), 두 시간 (two hours)'.

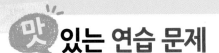 있는 연습 문제

1 Listen carefully and complete the sentences.

① 한국은 정말 _____.

② 명동까지 _____.

③ 오늘 날씨가 정말 _____.

④ 서울에서 부산까지 _____.

2 Complete the conversation as in |ex|.

> |ex| 가 **시험이 어려워요?**
>
> 나 **네.** 어려워요. (어렵다)

① 가 안나 씨 고향은 지금 겨울이에요?

　　나 네. 그래서 오늘도 _____. (춥다)

② 가 동생이 _____. 몇 살이에요? (귀엽다)

　　나 지금 다섯 살이에요.

③ 가 학교에서 집까지 어떻게 가요?

　　나 _____. (지하철 / 가다)

④ 가 집까지 얼마나 걸려요?

　　나 _____. (버스 / 한 시간쯤 걸리다)

*단어 Vocabulary　기차 train　　겨울 winter　　몇 how old　　살 age　　버스 bus

Transport in Korea

It is convenient in Korea with different mode of transports available. In large cities such as Seoul, Daegu and Busan, subways are well established, and you can travel around conveniently.

If you would like go to a place that is far away from Seoul, you can either take an express bus or by KTX. Express buses depart from Seoul, Gwangju, Busan, Daejeon, Jeonju, Cheonan and Daegu. The buses travel to various destinations via highway. You may get more information via the express bus service website (https://www.kobus.co.kr). You will be able to make a reservation, purchase a free pass voucher or make payment through their mobile app.

Some of the destinations do not have a non-stop bus service, then you may opt for buses with transit service. There are transit stops on major highways. Recently the premium express bus has been introduced and the seats are wider, and a screen is attached, hence it will make the journey more comfortable.

If you prefer to take the KTX, reservation can be made on the website (http://letskorail.com) or through mobile. Aside from reserving your KTX tickets, you may also purchase tickets for sightseeing with different themes.

With different mode of transportations available, it is really convenient to travel without a car in Korea.

우리 좀 쉴까요?

Shall we take a rest?

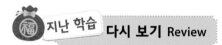

지난 학습 **다시 보기 Review**

♦ **KTX로 가세요.**

Go by KTX.

'N(으)로' is used to express a means, method, tool or direction for doing something.

- -

♦ **경주는 정말 아름다워요.**

Gyeongju is really beautiful.

When an adjective-stem or verb-stem ends in 'ㅂ' like in '어렵다(difficult), 귀엽다(cute), 무겁다(heavy)', the 'ㅂ' changes to '-오/우-' with an ending that starts in the vowel, '-아/어-' or '-았/었-'.

- Look at the following and answer O if it is correct or X if incorrect.

  ① 시험이 쉬어요.   (   )

  ② 명동까지 지하철으로 가세요.   (   )

  ③ 가방이 가벼워요.   (   )

Point

학습 포인트

☆ Learn the expressions to use when suggesting something.

☆ Learn expressions used to say that something happens one after another.

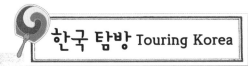

Have you heard of Jeonju? It is not only known as hanbok village but also famous for its creativity in food and has been recognized by UNESCO.

Bibimbap, Hanjeongsik (Korean table d'hôte) and bean sprout soup are especially popular here. Bibimbap is well known to foreigners, and they do have a festival devoted to that. Jeonju bibimbap contains a variety of delicious and healthy ingredients that are incomparable to other places' bibimbap in Korea. Bibimbap is also the representative of Korean food.

Other than bibimbap, Hanjeongsik is also highly recommended when you pay a visit to Jeonju. It is prepared with abundant ingredients such as seafood, meat and vegetables. It will be a different experience with the special table setting and amazing taste that would leave you with unforgettable memories.

Sentence
핵심 문장

17 우리 좀 쉴까요?
Shall we take a rest?

18 커피 한 잔 마시고 일해요.
Have a cup of coffee, and do work.

17 우리 좀 쉴까요?

Shall we take a rest?

✓ V-(으)ㄹ까요?

'-(으)ㄹ까요?' is used with a verb to suggest certain thing or to ask the listener's opinion by suggesting it.

	basic form	-(으)ㄹ까요?
Batchim O	앉다 sit	앉을까요? Shall we sit?
Batchim X	가다 go	갈까요? Shall we go?

ex 같이 영화를 볼까요? Shall we watch a movie together?

같이 쇼핑할까요? Shall we do the shopping together?

저녁에 치킨을 먹을까요? Shall we have fried chicken this evening?

가 주말에 같이 전주에 갈까요? Shall we go to Jeonju this weekend?

나 네. 좋아요. Yes. I am fine.

'-(으)ㄹ까요?' is used for a suggestion and there are many cases where the subject '우리(we)' is dropped. And the answer is usually ended in '-아요/어요'.

ex 가 (우리) 제주도에 갈까요? Shall we go to Jejudo Island?

나 네. 가요. Yes. Let's go.

🌸 **TIP** Koreans like to use words such as '같이(together)' or '함께(along with)'.
ex 우리 같이 산책할까요? Shall we take a walk together?

단어 **Vocabulary**

전주 Jeonju

140

Track 14-02

실력 다지기 Practice1

▶ Change the following words and fill in the blank.

	V-(으)ㄹ까요?
커피숍에 가다	커피숍에 갈까요?
밥을 먹다	
책을 읽다	
주말에 만나다	
공원에서 산책하다	
도서관에서 공부하다	

Track 14-03

실력 다지기 Practice2

▶ Practice the following as in |ex|.

|ex|
영화 / 보다 → 영화를 볼까요?

① 같이 / 축구 / 하다 → _____

② 같이 / 커피 / 마시다 → _____

③ 백화점 앞 / 만나다 → _____

④ 같이 / 학교 / 가다 → _____

단어 Vocabulary

커피숍 coffee shop   축구 soccer

18 커피 한 잔 마시고 일해요.

Have a cup of coffee, and do work.

✓ V-고

It indicates that a word(verb) with '-고' is followed by another word one after the other in time sequence.

	basic form	-고
Batchim O	먹다 eat	먹고 eat and
Batchim X	가다 go	가고 go and

ex 수업이 끝나고 집에 가요. The class is over and I'm going home.

밥을 먹고 숙제해요. I have some rice and do my homework.

드라마를 보고 운동하고 자요. I will watch drama first then do some exercises and finally go to bed.

If preceding and following words are switched, the meaning is changed.

밥을 먹고 물을 마셔요.	물을 마시고 밥을 먹어요.
I eat rice and drink water.	I drink water and eat rice.

Being attached to the end of an adjective or verb, it allows to add more words with different content.

ex 이 옷은 편하고 좋아요. This outfit is comfortable and good.

날씨가 맑고 따뜻해요. The weather is clear and warm.

저는 노래하고 동생은 춤을 춰요. I sing and my younger brother dances.

금요일에 공부하고 토요일에 아르바이트해요. I study on Friday and work part-time on Saturday.

단어 Vocabulary

끝나다 finish	드라마 drama	자다 sleep	편하다 comfortable
춤 dance	추다 dance	아르바이트하다 do a part-time job	

Track 14-05

▶ **실력 다지기 Practice3**

▶ Practice the following as in |ex|.

| ex |

샤워하다 + 텔레비전을 보다 → 샤워하고 텔레비전을 봤어요.

① 청소하다 + 쉬다 → _____

② 책을 읽다 + 커피를 마시다 → _____

③ 학교에서 공부하다 + 운동하다 → _____

④ 수업이 끝나다 + 노래방에 가다 → _____

▶ **실력 다지기 Practice4**

Track 14-06

▶ Practice the following as in |ex|.

| ex |

날씨가 따뜻하다 + 좋다 → 날씨가 따뜻하고 좋아요.

① 음식이 싸다 + 맛있다 → _____

② 동생이 귀엽다 + 예쁘다 → _____

③ 주말에 밥을 먹다 + 빵도 먹다 → _____

단어 Vocabulary

샤워하다 take a shower   텔레비전 TV   싸다 cheap

☀️ 피터와 또안이 일을 하고 있습니다.

피터	오늘은 일이 좀 많아요.[①]
또안	우리 좀 쉴까요?
피터	좋아요. 커피 한 잔 마시고 일해요.
또안	그런데 피터 씨, 다음 주에 어디로 출장을 가요?
피터	전주로 가요.

단어 Vocabulary

좀 a little
많다 lots of
쉬다 take a rest
일하다 work
다음 주 next week
출장 business trip

💬 Summarize the dialog.

① 두 사람은 지금 커피를 _____.

② 피터 씨는 다음 주에 _____.

☀ Peter and Doan are working.

Peter   I have a lot of work to do today.

Doan   Shall we take a rest?

Peter   Sure. Let's have a coffee and continue our work.

Doan   But Mr. Peter, where are you going for your business trip next week?

Peter   I'm going to Jeonju.

 맛있는 대화 **TIP**

① Most of the Korean companies work from Monday to Friday, starts at 9 in the morning and finishes at 6 in the evening. Working hours may vary from company to company, however there are cases where people have to work overtime when they have more work to complete. They might look busy all the time, but recently Korean companies have created different spaces for their employees to take a break so that they can rest in between.

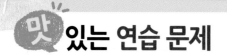

있는 연습 문제

1 Complete the conversation as in |ex|.

|ex| 가 **주말에 공원에서 산책할까요?** (산책하다)

나 **네. 좋아요.**

① 가 같이 테니스를 _____? (치다)

나 네. 좋아요.

② 가 저녁에 잠깐 _____? (만나다)

나 네. 어디에서 만나요?

③ 가 너무 심심해요.

나 영화를 _____? (보다)

④ 가 도서관에서 같이 _____? (공부하다)

나 네. 좋아요.

Track 14-08

2 Listen carefully and complete the sentence.

① _____ 숙제해요.

② _____ 샤워할 거예요.

③ _____ 여행 갈 거예요.

④ _____ 집에 갔어요.

*단어 Vocabulary 테니스 tennis   치다 play   잠깐 for a minute   심심하다 bored

Accommodation in Korea

Where do you usually stay when you travel? Many people usually stay in a hotel or guest house. But you can experience something different in Korea, to stay in a hanok (Korean traditional house). Hanoks are available not only in Seoul, but also in Gyeongju, Andong, Gongju Hanok Village and Jeonju Hanok Village.

The exterior retains the traditional design of a hanok, but there are many places where the interior has been refurbished and modern facilities fitted to make it comfortable for the guest. Aside from that, most of the hanoks are equipped with 'ondol', a traditional Korean floor heating system.

There are also many temples in Korea, where you can book to experience temple stay. It is worth a try if you would like to learn about the Buddhist culture and have some quiet time. Reservation can be made via the Temple Stay website (https://www.templestay.com). Take a look if this is something special you would like to try for your visit.

사진제공(브이앤드)
-한국관광공사

사진제공(브이앤드)-한국관광공사

셋째 주 다시 보기 DAY 11-14
Third week Review

이번 주 학습 내용 Lessons This Week –

DAY 11

◆ **V-(으)ㄹ 거예요** ▶ '-(으)ㄹ 거예요' is attached to the end of a verb, and it is used to indicate about a future plan.

> ⓔⓧ 저는 이따 커피를 마실 거예요. I will have a coffee later.
>
> 내일 책을 읽을 거예요. I will read a book tomorrow.

◆ **N하고** ▶ '하고' comes right after a personage-noun to describe that the person is grouped with someone/something together. By writing the form of 'N하고 N', you can connect each of the nouns as having the quivalent qualification.

> ⓔⓧ 민영 씨는 친구하고 도서관에서 공부해요. Minyoung is studying with her friend in the library.
>
> 또안 씨는 빵하고 우유를 먹어요. Doan is eating bread with milk.

DAY 12

◆ **V/A-았어요/었어요** ▶ '-았어요/었어요' is attached at the end of a verb or adjective to describe something happened in the past.

> ⓔⓧ 작년에 제주도에 여행 갔어요. I went on a trip to Jejudo Island last year.
>
> 어제 영화를 봤어요. 아주 재미있었어요. I watched a movie yesterday. It was really interesting.

◆ **V-고 싶다** ▶ '-고 싶다' comes at the end of a verb to say that you want something.

> ⓔⓧ 제주도에 가고 싶어요. I want to go to Jejudo Island.
>
> 치킨을 먹고 싶어요. I want to have fried chicken.

파이팅!

[1-2] Listen carefully and choose the correct answer to the question.

Track 15-01

1
① 저는 매일 공부해요.
② 친구하고 노래방에 갈 거예요.
③ 친구하고 커피숍에서 공부했어요.

2
① 쇼핑할 거예요.
② 친구를 만났어요.
③ 친구하고 이야기해요.

Track 15-02

3 Listen carefully and choose the same thing as in the conversation.

① 여자는 불고기를 먹을 거예요.
② 남자는 한국 음식을 좋아해요.
③ 여자는 주말에 친구를 만날 거예요.
④ 남자는 내일 친구하고 이야기할 거예요.

4 Read the following and answer the question.

> 저는 어제 친구하고 홍대에 갔어요. 쇼핑하고 구경했어요. 그리고 저녁에 삼겹살을 먹었어요. 정말 맛있었어요. 어제는 정말 즐거웠어요. 다음 주 주말에 친구하고 홍대에 또 갈 거예요.

Choose the same thing as in the writing.

① 이 사람은 지금 배가 고파요.
② 이 사람은 어제 홍대에서 쇼핑했어요.
③ 이 사람은 혼자 홍대에서 구경했어요.
④ 이 사람은 내일 삼겹살을 먹을 거예요.

*단어 Vocabulary 이야기하다 talk   여자 woman   홍대 Hongdae(Hongik Univ.)   구경하다 look around, sightsee
삼겹살 samgyeopsal(grilled pork belly)   즐겁다 fun   또 again, also   혼자 alone

DAY 13

◆ **N(으)로** ▶ It is used to express a means, method, tool or direction for doing something.

> (ex) 한국 사람은 젓가락으로 밥을 먹어요. Koreans eat with chopsticks.
>
> 지금 길이 막혀요. 지하철로 가세요. The road is blocked now. Go by subway.

◆ **'ㅂ' irregular** ▶ A Batchim 'ㅂ' changes to '-오/우-' before an ending stem with the vowel such as '-아/어-' or '-았/었-' when it, as a Batchim, is in an adjective like '덥다(hot), 어렵다(difficult), 맵다(spicy), 귀엽다(cute), etc.' as well as in a verb like '돕다(help), etc.'

> (ex) 오늘 좀 추워요. It's a little cold today.
>
> 가방이 무거워요. The bag is heavy.
>
> 윤기 씨는 친구를 잘 도와요. Yoonki is good at helping his friends.

DAY 14

◆ **V-(으)ㄹ까요?** ▶ '-(으)ㄹ까요?' attaches to the end of a verb to suggest something or ask for an opinion while suggesting it to the listener.

> (ex) 같이 영화를 볼까요? Shall we watch a movie together?
>
> 저녁에 치킨을 먹을까요? Shall we have fried chicken this evening?

◆ **V-고** ▶ It indicates that the preceding and following words occur one after the other after the verb.

> (ex) 수업이 끝나고 집에 가요. The class is over and I'm going home.
>
> 밥을 먹고 숙제해요. I have some rice and do my homework.

파이팅!

Track 15-03

1 Listen carefully and choose the same thing as in the conversation.

① 남자는 케이팝을 좋아해요.

② 여자는 금요일에 잠실에 갈 거예요.

③ 여자는 케이팝 콘서트를 볼 거예요.

④ 남자는 토요일에 노래를 할 거예요.

[2-3] Read the following and answer the question.

저는 등산을 좋아해요. 그래서 방학에 산에 자주 가요. 한국에서 설악산이 유명해요.

그래서 작년 여름에 친구하고 설악산에 갔어요. 등산하고 수영도 했어요.

이번 방학에도 설악산에 갈 거예요. 설악산에서 사진을 (㉠   ).

2 Choose the proper word for ㉠.

① 볼 거예요   ② 찍을 거예요

③ 만날 거예요   ④ 좋아할 거예요

3 Choose the same thing as in the writing.

① 이 사람은 오늘 산에 가요.

② 이 사람은 내일 산에 갈 거예요.

③ 이 사람은 방학에 등산을 할 거예요.

④ 이 사람은 지금 산에서 사진을 봐요.

*단어 Vocabulary 별일 a particular thing   왜 why   시 o'clock   케이팝 K-pop   잠실 Jamsil

역 station   등산 hike   산 mountain   설악산 Seoraksan Mountain

유명하다 famous   여름 summer   수영 swimming

★ 우리만 알고 있는

여행 이야기

The Travel Story that Only We Know

📷 If you want to experience the history and culture of Korea?

Gyeongju and Jeonju are the iconic places where you can experience the history and culture of the Korea.
You can experience the history in Gyeongju where historic trails can be seen everywhere in the city. Meanwhile in Jeonju, the Hanok Village is the spotlight of the city. Othwise, Hahoe Village in Andong, Gyeongsangbuk-do is also another place that worth to visit.

The village, called Andong Hahoe Village too, is a folk village that has preserved its tradition for more than 600 years. It is a place where you can understand the life of Koreans, and the locals have been protecting the traditional culture for a long time. It has also been recognised as a UNESCO World Heritage Site for its history. You will be able to watch various Korean traditional plays and the Korean special wedding ceremonies there.

On the other hand, Yeongwol where the Donggang River flows, is well-known for its beautiful Korean culture too. Every August, the 'Raft Festival' is held, and you would not want to miss it.

Korea through taste

If you have interest in Korean food, it will be exciting to try the different flavours of kimchi in each region. Besides kimchi, which is the representative of Korean food, there are also many delicious foods that worth a try. Be sure to try it out when you are in Korea!

🏅 경주 황남빵 Gyeongju Hwangnam Bread

Hwangnam bread, is an iconic food of Gyeongju-the historical city of Korea. It is a kind of bread fill with red bean paste in wheat flour dough. It is loved by most people due to its sweetness and it is a must-try food when you visit the city.

🏅 비빔밥 Bibimbap

Bibimbap is another classic food of Korea and it is famous in many other countries (maybe globally now) too. The ingredients for bibimbap differ from region to region. At a regional restaurant near the seaside, you can have bibimbap with seafood such as 'sea urchin bibimbap' or 'yukhoe (Korean-style raw beef) bibimbap'. Make sure you try at least one of those!

bibimbap

yukhoe bibimbap

sea urchin bibimbap

이렇게 말해요! Say like this!

Korean restaurants serve side dishes for free. If you want more side dishes, say the following.

반찬 좀 더 주세요.
Can I have more side dishes, please.

WEEK 04

한국의 관광 도시로 떠나요.
Let's go to a tourist city in Korea.

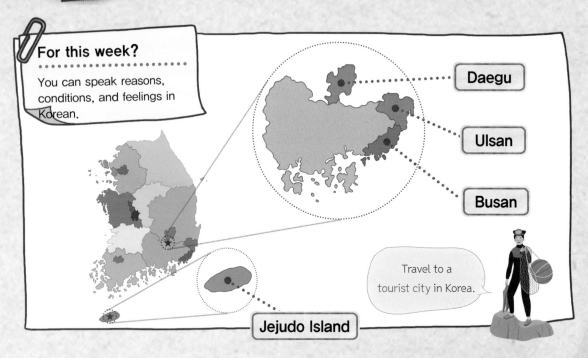

For this week?

You can speak reasons, conditions, and feelings in Korean.

Daegu

Ulsan

Busan

Jejudo Island

Travel to a tourist city in Korea.

DAY 16 관형형 말하기

Speaking in Determiner-form

관형형 말하기

DAY 17 이유 말하기

Speaking about reason

DAY 18 조건 표현하기
Expressing the conditions

DAY 19 느낌 말하기
Expressing the feelings

DAY 20

Fourth week DAY 16–19 Review

Review the main lessons of DAY 16–19, and check your Korean with various questions.

Travel & Culture in Korea

Explore Korea's tourist cities and learn about their representative cuisine.

DAY 16

관형형 말하기 Speaking in Determiner-form

정말 아름다운 곳이에요.

It's a really beautiful place.

지난 학습 다시 보기 Review

◆ **우리 좀 쉴까요?**

Shall we take a rest?

> '-(으)ㄹ까요?' attaches to the end of a verb to suggest something or ask for an opinion while suggesting it to the listener.

◆ **커피 한 잔 마시고 일해요.**

Have a cup of coffee, and do work.

> '-고' attaches to the end of a verb indicating that the word before and after occurs one after the other.

● Look at the following and answer O if it is correct or X if it is incorrect.

① 같이 밥을 먹을까요?　　　(　　　)

② 커피숍에서 공부할까요?　　(　　　)

③ 밥을 먹고 커피를 마셔요.　　(　　　)

학습 포인트 Point

☆ Learn the expression that modifies noun.

☆ Learn the expression for negation.

Daegu, one of Korea's metropolitan cities, has various gourmet meal such as 'makchang gui (grilled beef entrails)' and 'jjimgalbi (braised beef ribs)'. The city has a couple of nice things to enjoy too aside from food, like Dongseong-ro, Suseongmot Lake, the Mountain Sky Garden in Palgongsan, and Seomun Market.

The lake, Suseongmot, is a large one with a surface of about 2km and the night view is exceptionally beautiful. On the other hand, the Palgongsan Mountain, where you can take the cable car, is a stunning place to enjoy the panoramic view of Daegu city from the top.

And lastly, Daegu Seomun Market was one of the three largest markets during the Joseon Dynasty and it is still famous nowadays for its night market that is filled with delicious food and attractions.

Suseongmot Lake

makchang gui

Palgongsan Gatbawi

jjimgalbi

Sentence
핵심 문장

19 정말 아름다운 곳이에요.

It's a really beautiful place.

20 아침에 밥을 안 먹었어요.

I did not have breakfast this morning.

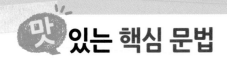

19 정말 아름다운 곳이에요.

It's a really beautiful place.

✓ A-(으)ㄴ / V-는 N

It comes at the end of an adjective or a verb in the determiner-form to decorate the following noun.

	basic form(A)	-(으)ㄴ N
Batchim O	좋다 good	좋은 사람 good person
Batchim X	예쁘다 pretty	예쁜 옷 pretty clothes

	basic form(V)	-는 N
Batchim O	먹다 eat	먹는 음식 food to eat
Batchim X	가다 go	가는 사람 a person going

ex 우리 언니는 정말 좋은 사람이에요. My sister is a nice person.

저는 어제 예쁜 가방을 샀어요. I bought a pretty bag yesterday.

제가 자주 가는 곳은 커피숍이에요. I often go to a coffee shop.

요즘 읽는 책이 재미있어요. I'm reading an interesting book nowadays.

> **TIP** 'ㅂ' irregular adjectives such as '어렵다(difficult), 무섭다(scary)' should be written '어려운, 무서운' in their determined form. And '맛있다(delicious), 맛없다(tasteless), 재미있다(fun)' is written as '맛있는, 맛없는, 재미있는' in the form.
>
> ex 이건 정말 어려운 문제예요. This is a really difficult question.
> 저는 무서운 영화를 싫어해요. I dislike a scary movie.
> 재미있는 영화를 보고 싶어요. I want to watch an interesting movie.

단어 Vocabulary

곳 place   문제 question, problem   무섭다 scary   싫어하다 dislike

▶ **실력 다지기 Practice1**

▶ Change the following words and fill in the blank.

	A–(으)ㄴ / V–는 N
매일 가다 + 커피숍	매일 가는 커피숍
좋아하다 + 책	
바쁘다 + 친구	
맛있다 + 음식	
무겁다 + 가방	

▶ **실력 다지기 Practice2**

▶ Complete the conversation as in |ex|.

|ex|　가　**이 책은 제가 좋아하는 책이에요.** (좋아하다)

　　　나　**재미있어요?**

① 가 저기에서 커피를 ＿＿＿＿＿＿＿＿ 사람은 누구예요? (마시다)

　 나 제 친구 윤기 씨예요.

② 가 어떤 영화를 좋아해요?

　 나 저는 ＿＿＿＿＿＿＿＿ 영화를 좋아해요. (슬프다)

③ 가 민영 씨는 정말 ＿＿＿＿＿＿＿＿ 사람이에요. (좋다)

　 나 고마워요.

④ 가 요즘 자주 ＿＿＿＿＿＿＿＿ 노래가 있어요? (듣다)

　 나 네. 저는 한국 노래를 많이 들어요.

단어 Vocabulary

어떤 certain　　　　슬프다 sad　　　　노래 song　　　　많이 much

20

아침에 밥을 안 먹었어요.

I did not have breakfast this morning.

✓ 안 V/A

'안' is used to express negative or opposite meaning by adding it in front of a verb or an adjective.

ex 민영 씨는 고기를 안 먹어요. Minyoung doesn't eat meat.

윤기 씨는 내일 모임에 안 올 거예요. Yoonki is not coming to the meeting tomorrow.

어제 피터 씨는 기분이 안 좋았어요. Peter was in bad mood yesterday.

TIP In the case of the verb '하다', you should use it in '공부 안 하다', not in '안 공부하다'.
ex 또안 씨는 오늘 일 안 해요. Doan is not working today.
안나 씨는 노래 안 해요. Anna doesn't sing.

TIP We say the verb '좋아하다(like)' as '안 좋아하다' for its negative form. So does the adjective '깨끗하다(clean)' as '안 깨끗하다' as well as the one '조용하다(quiet)' as '안 조용하다' for each negative form with the same pattern like in the above verb.

 단어 Vocabulary

고기 meat   모임 meeting

◖ 실력 다지기 Practice3 ◗

▶ Change the following words and fill in the blank.

	안 V/A
학교에 가다	학교에 안 가요
집에 오다	
술을 마시다	
책을 읽다	
청소하다	
비싸다	
따뜻하다	

◖ 실력 다지기 Practice4 ◗

▶ Practice the following as in |ex|.

| ex | **밥을 먹다** → 밥을 안 먹었어요.

① 길이 막히다 → _____

② 마음에 들다 → _____

③ 케이크를 만들다 → _____

④ 시험이 끝나다 → _____

◖ 단어 ◗ Vocabulary

술 alcohol

 **있는 대화**

☀ 또안과 윤기가 대구에 갔습니다.

또안　　대구는 처음이에요. 정말 아름다운 곳이에요.

윤기　　네. 여기는 제가 좋아하는 곳이에요.

　　　　작년 휴가 때에도 왔어요.

또안　　그런데 배가 좀 고파요. 아침에 밥을 안 먹었어요.①

윤기　　벌써 11시②예요. 우리 밥을 먹을까요?

　　　　여기에 맛있는 음식도 많아요.

단어 Vocabulary

대구 Daegu
처음 first time
곳 place
작년 last year
휴가 vacation
때 time
아침 morning
벌써 already
시 o'clock

💬 Summarize the dialog.

① 대구는 _____ 곳이에요.

② 또안 씨는 밥을 _____.

162

☀ Doan and Yoonki went to Daegu.

Doan   This is my first time in Daegu. It's a really beautiful place.

Yoonki   Yes. This is my favorite place.

         I came here last year for vacation too.

Doan   But I'm a little hungry. I didn't have breakfast this morning.

Yoonki   It's already 11 o'clock. Shall we have some food?

         There are a lot of delicious food here.

 맛있는 대화 TIP

① It is important to Koreans to have breakfast everyday. However, nowadays Koreans tend to skip breakfast due to their busy schedule. In tradition, it is important to have a good breakfast as it is the best way to start your day healthily.

② When we are telling time, we say "한 시(1 o'clock), 두 시(2 o'clock), 세 시(3 o'clock), 네 시(4 o'clock), 다섯 시(5 o'clock), 여섯 시(6 o'clock)", and when telling time in minutes, we say "일 분(1 minute), 십 분(10 minutes), 삼십 분(30 minutes)".

맛있는 연습 문제

1 Listen carefully and complete the sentences.

Track 16-08

① 제가 ＿＿＿＿＿＿＿＿＿＿＿ 만들었어요.

② 저는 ＿＿＿＿＿＿＿＿＿＿＿ 싫어해요.

③ 요즘 ＿＿＿＿＿＿＿＿＿＿＿ 있어요?

④ 윤기 씨는 제가 정말 ＿＿＿＿＿＿＿＿＿＿＿.

2 Complete the conversation as in |ex|.

| ex | 가 그 이야기 윤기 씨한테 하지 마세요.
    나 네. 안 할 거예요.

① 가 술을 마셔요?

　　나 아니요. ＿＿＿＿＿＿＿＿＿＿＿.

② 가 어제 민영 씨를 만났어요?

　　나 아니요. ＿＿＿＿＿＿＿＿＿＿＿.

③ 가 파티에 갈 거예요?

　　나 아니요. ＿＿＿＿＿＿＿＿＿＿＿.

④ 가 이번 공연에서 노래해요?

　　나 아니요. ＿＿＿＿＿＿＿＿＿＿＿.

*단어 Vocabulary　사랑하다 love　한테 to, for　이번 this time　공연 concert

164

Korean public holidays

Do you know when the public holidays are in Korea? Usually, they are set by the government and include the national holidays and anniversaries when people do not work or go to school. Korean New Year's Day, the first day of January on the lunar calendar, and Chuseok (the 15th day of August on the lunar calendar), Korean Thanksgiving Day, are mainly the most important holidays in Korea. I usually spend about three days relaxing and spending time with my family. Usually, restaurants, shops and department stores are closed during these holidays.

The public holidays also include Children's Day (5th May) and Hangeul Day (9th October) to commemorate and celebrate the special day.

If the public holiday falls on a Friday or Monday, most of the shops are closed from Friday to Sunday or from Saturday to Monday, which is known as a long holiday or long weekend. I would usually rest at home or go on a short trip nearby.

Sometimes people will go on long vacations on holidays. They would either travel domestically or sometimes go abroad. The peak season for vacation is from mid-July to mid-August during the hot summer months. In Korea, people go for a holiday at different times, but most people would choose to take a break when it is hot in summer. The cost of traveling will usually surge during the peak season.

그냥 심심해서 전화했어요.
I called just because I was bored.

지난 학습 **다시 보기 Review**

◆ **정말 아름다운 곳이에요.** ⤳ '-(으)ㄴ, -는' comes to decorate the following noun at the end of an adjective or a verb in its determiner-form.

It's a really beautiful place.

- -

◆ **아침에 밥을 안 먹었어요.** ⤳ '안' is used to express negative or opposite meaning by adding it in front of a verb or an adjective.

I did not have breakfast this morning.

◆ Look at the following and answer O if it is correct or X if incorrect.

① 여기는 재미있는 곳이에요.　　　(　　　)

② 저 영화는 정말 무섭은 영화예요.　(　　　)

③ 형은 안 공부해요.　　　　　　　(　　　)

Point

학습 포인트

☆ Learn the expression to speak the reason.

☆ Learn the expression to speak what I am doing now.

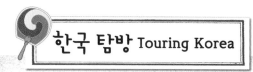
한국 탐방 Touring Korea

There are many attractive places in Ulsan. Every New Year's Day, lots of people watch the sunrise at Ganjeolgot Cape, the famous spot for watching it. Also, there is the world's biggest post box in it, so it would be nice to send a letter from there to your loved ones.

Ulsan is also an area where they can catch many whales. Therefore, they call it the Whale Culture Village. You can find many things about whales there.

Aside from that, you can also visit the Daewangam Park, where you can enjoy the beauty of the East Sea, and the Yeongnam Alps, where there are nine mountains.

Ganjeolgot Cape

Daewangam Park

Yeongnam Alps

Sentence
핵심 문장

21 그냥 심심해서 전화했어요.
I called just because I was bored.

22 여기저기 구경하고 있어요.
I'm touring here.

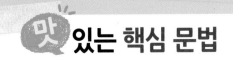

21 그냥 심심해서 전화했어요.

I called just because I was bored.

✓ V/A-아서/어서

'-아서/어서' is applicable at the end of a verb or an adjective to explain the reason or ground.

	basic form		-아서/어서	
ㅏ, ㅗ	앉다 sit		앉다 + 아서	앉아서
The others	맛있다 delicious		맛있다 + 어서	맛있어서
하다	공부하다 study		공부하다	공부해서

ex 그 영화가 재미있어서 두 번 봤어요. I watched the movie twice because it was funny.

날씨가 좋아서 공원에서 산책했어요. I took a walk in the park because the weather was nice.

저는 커피를 좋아해서 많이 마셔요. I drink a lot of coffee because I like it.

TIP In reason speaking cannot '-(으)세요' or '-(으)ㄹ까요?' come right after the verb-stem.

ex 비가 와서 우산을 가지고 가세요. (×)
비가 와서 우산을 가지고 갔어요. (○) I took an umbrella because it was raining.
배가 아파서 병원에 갈까요? (×)
배가 아파서 병원에 가요. (○) I went to the hospital because my stomach hurt.

TIP Should a verb including '-아서/어서'(ex: of simple past) come before a verb including '-았/었'(ex: of more past) in the timely lineal sequence of the sentence.

ex 비가 왔어서 우산을 샀어요. (×)
비가 와서 우산을 샀어요. (○) I bought an umbrella because it was raining.

TIP When combining a noun, it is said as '이어서/여서' or '(이)라서'.

ex 내일은 토요일이어서 수업이 없어요. There is no class because it is Saturday tomorrow.
= 내일은 토요일이라서 수업이 없어요.
그 친구는 가수여서 노래를 잘해요. Because that friend is a singer, he sings a song well.
= 그 친구는 가수라서 노래를 잘해요.

단어 Vocabulary

번 time, number   비가 오다 rain   가지다 take

Track 17-02

◀█ 실력 다지기 Practice1 █▶

▶ Practice the following as in |ex|.

|ex|
배가 고프다 + 밥을 먹다 → 배가 고파서 밥을 먹었어요.

① 사과가 싸다 + 많이 사다   → _____

② 날씨가 춥다 + 집에 있다   → _____

③ 커피를 많이 마시다 + 잠이 안 오다 → _____

◀█ 실력 다지기 Practice2 █▶

▶ Select the most suitable word from |ex| to complete the conversation.
Track 17-03

|ex|
도와주다   길이 막히다   너무 재미있다

① 가 왜 이렇게 늦었어요?

　나 _____ 늦었어요. 미안해요.

② 가 그 책을 또 읽어요?

　나 네. _____ 또 읽어요.

③ 가 이사 준비가 다 끝났어요. _____ 고마워요.

　나 아니에요.

💬 단어 Vocabulary

잠 sleep　　　　　　　도와주다 help　　　　　왜 why　　　　　　이렇게 like this
늦다 late　　　　　　　또 again, also　　　　　이사 move　　　　　준비 preparation
다 all

22 여기저기 구경하고 있어요.

I'm touring here.

✓ V-고 있다

'-고 있다' is applicable at the end of a verb to describe an action continuing without an end.

	basic form	-고 있다
Batchim O	먹다 eat	먹고 있다 eating
Batchim X	가다 go	가고 있다 going

ex 안나 씨는 한국어를 공부하고 있어요. Anna is studying Korean language.

민영 씨는 지금 케이크를 만들고 있어요. Minyoung is making a cake now.

지금 윤기 씨가 피터 씨를 기다리고 있어요. Yoonki is waiting for Peter now.

🌸 **TIP** 'V-고 있다' is not combined with a verb that finishes in a moment such as '앉다(sit), 서다(stand), 죽다(die)'.
ex 동생이 앉고 있다. (×)

🌸 **TIP** 'V-고 있다' comes with a verb such as '살다(live)' or '배우다(learn)' to say that the situation is continuing.
ex 저는 지금 한국에 살고 있어요. I am living in Korea now.
안나 씨는 요즘 한국어를 배우고 있어요. Anna is learning Korean these days.

Track 17-05

실력 다지기 Practice3

▶ Change the following words and fill in the blank.

	V-고 있어요
집에 가다	집에 가고 있어요
책을 읽다	
집에서 쉬다	
공원에서 산책하다	
도서관에서 공부하다	

Track 17-06

실력 다지기 Practice4

▶ Complete the conversation as in |ex|.

|ex| 가 지금 뭐 해요?

나 **친구하고** 이야기하고 있어요. (이야기하다)

① 가 윤기 씨는 뭐 해요?

나 텔레비전을 _____. (보다)

② 가 여보세요? 피터 씨, 지금 어디예요?

나 명동이에요. 또안 씨하고 _____. (구경하다)

③ 가 지금 뭐 해요?

나 휴대 전화가 없어서 지금 휴대 전화를 _____. (찾다)

④ 가 윤기 씨, 왜 안 와요?

나 미안해요. 지금 _____. (가다)

단어 Vocabulary

여보세요 hello   찾다 find, search

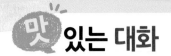 **있는 대화**

☀ 윤기와 민영이 전화합니다.

윤기	여보세요?① 민영 씨, 지금 어디예요?②
민영	울산에 왔어요. 무슨 일③ 있어요?
윤기	그냥 심심해서 전화했어요. 울산에서 뭐 해요?
민영	안나 씨하고 여기저기 구경하고 있어요.
	연휴라서 사람도 많아요.
윤기	그래요? 여행 잘 하고 오세요.

단어 Vocabulary

울산 Ulsan
무슨 what
그냥 just
심심하다 bored
전화하다 call
여기저기 here and there
구경하다 look around, sightsee
연휴 holiday

💬 Summarize the dialog.

① 민영 씨는 안나 씨하고 울산에 _____.

② 민영 씨는 지금 여기저기 _____.

☀ Yoonki and Minyoung are talking on the phone.

Yoonki	Hello? Ms. Minyoung, where are you now?
Minyoung	I am in Ulsan, now. Is there anything?
Yoonki	I called just because I was bored. What are you doing in Ulsan?
Minyoung	Ms. Anna and I are touring here.
	It's a holiday, hence there are many people.
Yoonki	Really? Enjoy your trip.

 맛있는 대화 **TIP**

① '여보세요?' is a greeting phrase when calling someone.

② It means 'where are you?' when asking someone '어디예요?'. You can then answer with '집이에요.(I am at home.)' or '한강 공원이에요.(I am at Hangang Park.)'.

③ Pronunciation: 무슨 일[무슨닐]

맛있는 연습 문제

1 Complete the conversation as in |ex|.

| ex | 가 **많이 기다렸어요? 늦어서 미안해요.** (늦다)

나 **괜찮아요. 저도 방금 왔어요.**

① 가 주말에 뭐 할 거예요?

나 동생이 _____ 같이 병원에 갈 거예요. (아프다)

② 가 어제 뭐 했어요?

나 시험이 _____ 공부했어요. (있다)

③ 가 어제 늦잠을 _____ 약속 시간에 늦었어요. (자다)

나 왜 늦잠을 잤어요? 또 드라마 봤어요?

④ 가 주말에 산에 갔어요?

나 아니요. 비가 _____ 안 갔어요. (오다)

Track 17-08

2 Listen carefully and complete the sentence.

① 동생은 지금 책을 _____.

② 요즘 한국어를 _____.

③ 형은 지금 _____.

*단어 Vocabulary   괜찮다 fine, ok   방금 just   늦잠 oversleep   약속 promise

First day of New Year

How do you usually spend the last or first day of the year?

In Korea, the bell rings at 00:00 on the last day of the year. The bell-ringing event is held at various locations, such as Bosingak Pavilion in Jongno-gu, Seoul, Busan, Daegu, Ulsan and Guangju. Many people would gather to watch the event. For public safety, the roads are controlled and the public transports (buses) run on diverted routes. In Seoul, the bell-ringing event is broadcast and there would be a concert either before or after the event.

Bosingak Pavilion

Koreans believe that if you watch the first sunrise of the year and make a wish while watching it, your wish will come true. There are a few amazing spots for viewing, such as Palgakjeong Pavilion in Namsan Mountain in Seoul, Jeongdongjin in Gangwon-do, Homigot Cape in Pohang, and Ganjeolgot Cape in Ulsan. Each region hosts various sunrise events and some of them even offer a 'Sunrise Train Travel' package. So why not give it a go and have a different start for the year. Don't forget to bring some warm clothes with you as winter in Korea can be cold!

Palgakjeong Pavilion

Jeongdongjin

Homigot Cape

DAY 18

조건 표현하기 Expressing the conditions

안나가 오면 출발하자.
Let's go when Anna comes.

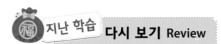

지난 학습 다시 보기 Review

◆ **그냥 심심해서 전화했어요.** ⟶ '–아서/어서' is applicable at the end of a verb or an adjective to explain the reason or ground.

I called just because I was bored.

◆ **여기저기 구경하고 있어요.** ⟶ '–고 있다' is applicable at the end of a verb to describe an action continuing without an end.

I'm touring here.

◆ Look at the following and answer O if it is correct or X if incorrect.

① 피터 씨는 지금 친구를 기다리고 있어요.　　(　　　)

② 같이 가고 싶어서 갈까요?　　(　　　)

③ 피곤해서 집에서 쉬었어요.　　(　　　)

Point
학습 포인트

☆ Learn the casual speech expression.

☆ Learn the expression of suggestion and condition.

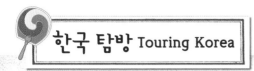
한국 탐방 Touring Korea

Busan is a city that you must visit when you are in Korea. In Songdo, there is a tourist spot named Songdo Marine Cable Car where you can take a ride and enjoy the view of the seashore to Amnam Park. From the Sky Habor Observatory, you can get a better overview of the seaside.

Also, try to walk the Yonggung Cloud Bridge. Or take a slow walk from Taejongdae to Oryukdo Sky Walk. The walkway finishes at Gamcheon Culture Village.

Aside from these, Haeundae Beach is the iconic beach where many people would gather every year. It is worth visiting Gwangalli Beach and Songdo Cloud Trail of Songdo Beach.

There are many things to enjoy in Busan, and I am sure you would love it.

Taejongdae

Haeundae Beach

Gamcheon Culture Village

Oryukdo Sky Walk

Sentence
핵심 문장

23 안나는 언제 와?
When is Anna coming?

24 안나가 오면 출발하자.
Let's go when Anna comes.

맛있는 핵심 문법

23 안나는 언제 와?

When is Anna coming?

✓ Casual speech

It is used for an informal and light tone when the speaker and listener have close relationship.

	basic form	−아/어	
ㅏ, ㅗ	만나다 meet	만나다 + 아	만나
The others	맛있다 delicious	맛있다 + 어	맛있어
하다	공부하다 study	공부하다	공부해

In '−아요/어요', you can use the form and leave out '요'.

−아요/어요 → −아/어	
가요	가
좋아요	좋아

−았어요/었어요 → −았어/었어	
먹었어요	먹었어
피곤했어요	피곤했어

−(으)ㄹ 거예요 → −(으)ㄹ 거야	
만날 거예요	만날 거야
공부할 거예요	공부할 거야

이에요/예요 → (이)야	
가방이에요	가방이야
친구예요	친구야

ex 가 어제 뭐 했어? What did you do yesterday?

나 친구를 만났어. I met my friend.

가 주말에 뭐 할 거야? What are you going to do on the weekend?

나 집에서 쉴 거야. I will take a rest at home.

TIP You can say casually in '응' as '네(Yes)', in '나' as '저(I)'and '내' as '제(my)'.
ex 가 같이 갈까? Shall we go together?
나 응, 나도 좋아. Yes, I would like it too.

TIP When you suggest to your close person in casual speech, use 'V−자'.
ex 가 같이 노래방에 가자. Let's go to the karaoke together.
나 응, 좋아. Yes, that sounds good.

실력 다지기 Practice1

▶ Change the following word into its casual speech.

	Casual speech
학교에 가요.	학교에 가.
집에 왔어요.	
커피를 마실 거예요.	
책을 읽을까요?	
청소하고 있어요.	
비싸요.	
따뜻해요.	
제 휴대 전화예요.	

실력 다지기 Practice2

▶ Practice the following as in | ex |.

> | ex | **친구 / 만나다** → 친구를 만나.

① 가방 / 무겁다 → _____

② 테니스 / 치다 → _____

③ 공원 / 산책하다 → _____

④ 한국 노래 / 좋아하다 → _____

24 안나가 오면 출발하자.

Let's go when Anna comes.

✓ V/A-(으)면

'-(으)면' comes at the end of a verb or an adjective assuming the situation or indicating that the preceding content becomes the basis or condition for the following.

	basic form	-(으)면
Batchim O	좋다 good	좋으면 if good
Batchim X	가다 go	가면 if go

ex 시간이 있으면 우리 집에 오세요. Come to my house when you have time.

돈이 많으면 뭐 하고 싶어요? What do you want to do when you have a lot of money?

한국에 오면 연락하세요. Please contact me if you are coming to Korea.

피곤하면 집에 가서 쉬세요. Please go home and take a rest if you are tired.

💡 **TIP** For 'ㅂ' irregular word, such as '덥다(hot), 가볍다(light)', write '더우면, 가벼우면', and if the Batchim ends in 'ㄹ' like '만들다(make), 살다(live), 힘들다(hard)', write only '면'.

ex 날씨가 추우면 여행을 안 가요. I do not travel if the weather is cold.

너무 더우면 에어컨을 켜세요. Switch on the air conditioner if it is too hot.

힘들면 쉬세요. Take a rest if you are exhausted.

케이크를 다 만들면 같이 먹어요. We can eat the cake together if we make it.

단어 Vocabulary

돈 money   연락하다 contact   에어컨 air conditioner   켜다 turn on

실력 다지기 Practice3

▶ Practice the following as in |ex|.

> |ex|
> 비가 오다 + 여행을 안 가다 → 비가 오면 여행을 안 갈 거예요.

① 날씨가 좋다 + 공원에 가다 → _____

② 시험이 끝나다 + 부산에서 여행하다 → _____

③ 한국에 가다 + 이태원에서 밥을 먹다 → _____

실력 다지기 Practice4

▶ Complete the conversation as in |ex|.

> |ex| 가 **많이 힘들어요? 힘들면 좀 쉬세요.** (힘들다)
>
> 나 **아니에요. 괜찮아요.**

① 가 다음에 또 _____ 안 돼요. (늦다)

  나 네. 다음에는 안 늦을 거예요.

② 가 내일 또 공원에서 운동할 거예요?

  나 날씨가 _____ 운동할 거예요. (괜찮다)

③ 가 몇 시에 도착해요?

  나 지금 _____ 7시에 도착해요. (출발하다)

단어 Vocabulary

이태원 Itaewon   안 되다 should not   도착하다 arrive

 있는 대화

 Track 18-07

☀ 또안이 민영을 기다려서 만났습니다.

민영   또안 씨, 오래 기다렸어요?

또안   아니요. 저도 방금 왔어요.

민영   그런데 이제 우리 말을 놓을까요?①

또안   좋아요. 아니, 좋아.

민영   그래.② 나도 좋아. 그런데 안나는 언제 와?

또안   곧 올 거야. 안나가 오면 출발하자.

💬 Summarize the dialog.

① 또안과 민영은 말을 _____ –았어요/었어요.

② 두 사람은 안나를 _____.

☀ Doan waited for Minyoung for their meeting.

Minyoung	Have you been waiting for a long time, Mr. Doan?
Doan	No. I have just arrived too, Ms. Minyoung.
Minyoung	Well, shall we speak casually to each other?
Doan	Yes. No, I mean yea.
Minyoung	Yea! I like this better. By the way, when is Anna coming?
Doan	She'll be here soon. Let's go when Anna comes.

 맛있는 대화 TIP

① When two individuals become close friends and wish to speak casually to each other, you can say, "말을 놓을까요?(Shall we speak casually to each other?)" or "우리 말 편하게 할까요?(Shall we speak comfortably?)".

② '그래요(yes), 그래(yea)' is an expression used when you agree with the other person's opinion.

맛있는 연습 문제

1 Change the following conversation into its casual speech.

> 또안 대구는 처음이에요. 정말 아름다운 곳이에요.
>
> 윤기 맞아요. 여기는 제가 자주 오는 곳이에요.
>
> 그런데 배가 좀 고파요. 아침에 밥을 안 먹었어요.
>
> 또안 그럼 먼저 밥을 먹을까요?
>
> 윤기 네. 여기에 맛있는 음식도 많아요.

↓

> 또안 대구는 ①_____. 정말 아름다운 ②_____.
>
> 윤기 ③_____. 여기는 ④_____ 자주 오는 ⑤_____.
>
> 그런데 배가 좀 고파. 아침에 밥을 ⑥_____.
>
> 또안 그럼 먼저 밥을 ⑦_____?
>
> 윤기 ⑧_____. 여기에 맛있는 음식도 많아.

2 Listen carefully and complete the sentences.

① _____ 산책할 거예요.

② _____ 집에서 쉬세요.

③ _____ 여행을 할 거예요.

④ _____ 배가 아파요.

*단어 Vocabulary 먼저 first   아이스크림 ice cream   많이 much

Casual speech and honorifics

In Korean, the choice of words and sentence endings are different according to the age or status of the person you are speaking to. Between close friends, you can speak casually (informally). It often depends on the relationship of two individuals, regardless the age. For example, if you are two years elder than the person you are speaking to, both of you can still speak casually if you have a close relationship.

When two individuals have a close relationship, it is quite natural to speak casually. However, either one would usually ask as a courtesy before they both start to speak informally, such as '말을 놓을까요?(Shall we speak casually to each other?)' and '이제 말을 놓으면 어떨까요?(How about us speaking informally?)'.

But, you should not use a casual speech on everyone. There are honorifics that you should keep and apply when speaking to an elder person or a person with a higher status. In the Korean language, honorific words are used by adding the '-시-' element, for example '식사 하세요, 식사하셨어요, 식사하실 거예요'.

In a workspace, if a subordinate continues to use honorifics when speaking, a person with a higher position may express his/her intention to speak casually by using the phrase '말씀 편하게 하세요(Take it easy)'.

DAY 19

느낌 말하기 Expressing the feelings

여기는 정말 예쁘네.
It's really pretty here.

지난 학습 **다시 보기 Review**

♦ **안나는 언제 와?**
When is Anna coming?

> Casual speech is used for an informal and light tone when the speaker and listener have close relationship.

♦ **안나가 오면 출발하자.**
Let's go when Anna comes.

> '-(으)면' comes at the end of a verb or an adjective assuming the situation or indicating that the preceding content becomes the basis or condition for the following.

● Look at the following and answer O if it is correct or X if incorrect.

① 같이 영화를 볼까?   (   )

② 지금 공부하.   (   )

③ 배고파면 밥 먹자.   (   )

Point
학습 포인트

☆ Learn the expression to say feelings.

☆ Learn the expression to deny certain things.

Most people would choose Jeju as the representative travel destination in Korea. There are various tourist spots to visit, such as Hallasan Mountain, Seongsan Ilchulbong Peak, Seopjikoji Hill, Cheonjeyeon Waterfall, Hyeopjae Beach and Hamdeok Beach. Aside from natural scenic spots, there are many museums with theme too.

You will not only able to enjoy the beauty of nature and museums, but you would also indulge yourself with delicious food in Jeju. They are especially famous for their black pork samgyeopsal (grilled pork belly), and also cutlassfish dishes, noodles served with different types of meat, and more!

We believe it will be a fruitful trip for everyone and why not get freshen up now at the amazing Jeju!

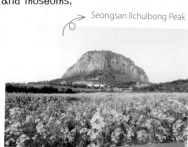

Seongsan Ilchulbong Peak

Udo Island

Cheonjeyeon Waterfall

dolhareubang

Sentence 핵심 문장

25 여기는 정말 예쁘네.

It's really pretty here.

26 지난번에 비가 많이 와서 못 갔어.

I could not go because it was raining last time.

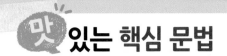 있는 핵심 문법

 Track 19-01

25 여기는 정말 예쁘네.

It's really pretty here.

✓ V/A-네요

'-네요' is used when the speaker talks about a new fact learned now through direct experience or something else.

	basic form	-네요
Batchim O	좋다 good	좋네요 It is good
Batchim X	가다 go	가네요 It goes

ex 오늘 날씨가 정말 춥네요. The weather is cold today.

여기는 사람이 많네요. There are many people here.

안나 씨는 한국말을 잘하네요. Anna speaks Korean well.

가 코트가 잘 어울리네요. The coat looks good on you.

나 고마워요. Thank you.

TIP 'ㄹ' is dropped in a word with the stem 'ㄹ Batchim' like in '살다(live), 만들다(make), 멀다(be far away)', so you can get the form like '사네요, 만드네요, 머네요'.
  ex 가 학교에서 집까지 한 시간 반 걸려요. It takes an hour and a half from school to home.
    나 집이 머네요. Your home is far away.

TIP ① Don't use '저(I)' as a subject if it indicates the truth that you get to know now.
    ex 제가 집에 가네요. (×)

② Concerning the truth of the past, say '-았네요/었네요'.
    ex 이번 공연에 사람이 정말 많이 왔네요. A lot of people came to this show.

단어 Vocabulary

코트 coat   어울리다 look good on   반 half

실력 다지기 Practice1

▶ Change the following words and fill in the blank.

	–네요
책을 많이 읽다	책을 많이 읽네요
운동을 잘하다	
눈이 많이 오다	
날씨가 맑다	
시험이 어렵다	
동생이 예쁘다	

실력 다지기 Practice2

▶ Complete the conversation as in |ex|.

| ex | 가 이 집 케이크가 맛있어요.

나 맞아요. 정말 맛있네요. (맛있다)

① 가 경치가 정말 _____. (아름답다)

　나 네. 정말 좋아요.

② 가 윤기 씨는 책을 정말 많이 _____. (읽다)

　나 그냥 책을 좋아해요.

③ 가 일찍 _____. (오다)

　나 네. 일이 빨리 끝났어요.

④ 가 청소를 다 _____. (하다)

　나 네. 방금 다 했어요.

단어 Vocabulary

눈 snow   일찍 early   빨리 quickly   방금 just

26 지난번에 비가 많이 와서 못 갔어.

I could not go because it was raining last time.

✓ 못 V

'못' comes in front of a verb to say that the verb cannot perform its action.

	basic form	못
Batchim O	먹다 eat	못 먹어요 can't eat
Batchim X	가다 go	못 가요 can't go

ex 저는 춤을 못 춰요. I cannot dance.

제 동생은 테니스를 못 쳐요. My younger brother cannot play tennis.

일이 많아서 집에 일찍 못 가요. I cannot go home early because I have a lot of work.

어제 커피를 많이 마셔서 잠을 못 잤어요. I could not sleep because I drank a lot of coffee yesterday.

TIP In case of '하다' verb, you use the form of '공부 못 해요'.
> **ex** 저는 노래 못 해요. I can't sing.
> 아파서 청소를 못 했어요. I couldn't do cleaning because I was sick.

TIP '못' is used only in front of a verb, but '안' can be used for both verb and adjective.
'못' indicated incompetence, but '안' means simple negation. Use '못' if you wish to do something you can't do.
> **ex** 숙제가 너무 어려웠어요. 그리고 시간도 없었어요. 그래서 숙제를 못 했어요.
> The homework was too difficult. I had no time too. So I could not do my homework.
> 시간이 있었어요. 하지만 숙제를 안 했어요. I had time. But I did not do my homework.

TIP When pronouncing, be careful.
> **ex** 못 해요[모태요]   못 가요[몯까요]   못 먹어요[몬머거요]

실력 다지기 Practice3

▶ Change the following words and fill in the blank.

	못
책을 읽다	책을 못 읽어요
영화를 보다	
술을 마시다	
친구를 만나다	
운동하다	
청소하다	

실력 다지기 Practice4

▶ Complete the conversation as in |ex|.

|ex|　가　왜 밥 안 먹었어요?

　　　나　바빠서 못 먹었어요.

① 가 왜 파티에 안 갔어요?

　　나 머리가 너무 아파서 _____.

② 가 그 모자 왜 안 사요?

　　나 사고 싶지만 너무 비싸서 _____.

③ 가 숙제 다 했어요?

　　나 아니요. 친구가 우리 집에 와서 _____.

④ 가 스키를 타요?

　　나 아니요. _____.

단어 Vocabulary

스키 | skiing

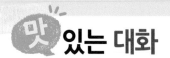

☀ 민영과 안나가 제주도에 갔습니다.

민영   여기는 정말 예쁘네.

안나   응. 그런데 커플①도 정말 많네.

민영   하하. 여기는 드라마에도 많이 나왔어.

       우리 내일은 우도②에 갈까?

안나   좋아. 이번에 우도에 꼭 갈 거야.

       지난번에 비가 많이 와서 못 갔어.

단어   Vocabulary
커플 couple
하하 haha
드라마 drama
나오다 appear
우도 Udo Island
이번 this time
꼭 definitely
지난번 last time

🍈 Summarize the dialog.

① 두 사람이 지금 있는 곳은 드라마에도 _____.

② 안나 씨는 지난번에 _____ –아서/어서 우도에 _____.

192

☼ Minyoung and Anna went to Jejudo Island.

Minyoung   It's really pretty here.

Anna   Yes. There are many couples here too.

Minyoung   Haha. Many dramas were filmed here.

           Shall we go to Udo Island tomorrow?

Anna   Sure. I definitely want to go to Udo Island this time.

           I could not go because it was raining last time.

 맛있는 대화 **TIP**

① Korean couples wear couple rings, same T-shirts or sneakers most of the time. Wearing the
   same clothes or accessories is a form of expression of love for each other.

② Udo Island is well-known for its beautiful scenery and it is comparable to Jeju! You can go to
   Udo Island by boat from Jeju and peanut ice cream is famous there. So give it a try!

있는 연습 문제

1 Complete the conversation as in |ex|.

|ex| 가 동생이에요? 정말 귀엽네요. (귀엽다)

나 고마워요.

① 가 배가 좀 _____. (고프다)

나 그럼 우리 뭐 먹을까요?

② 가 너무 _____. (심심하다)

나 맞아요. 영화 볼까요?

③ 가 열심히 _____. (공부하다)

나 다음 주에 시험이 있어요.

Track 19-08

2 Listen carefully and complete the sentences.

① 저는 운동을 _____.

② 제 친구는 고기를 _____.

③ 잠을 _____ 너무 피곤해요.

④ 수영을 _____ 수영장에 안 가요.

*단어 Vocabulary   열심히 hard   잠 sleep   수영장 swimming pool

KOREA

Jejudo Island's Jeongnang

Jejudo is also known as 'Samdado' for its stones, strong winds, and women since the olden times. You will often see the stone walls and the strong wind blowing all the time on Jejudo Island. There is an old saying that most men worked at the sea and women were left alone in Jeju when their men suffered from unforeseeable circumstances.

Due to the all-time strong wind in Jeju, you will see the roof of a traditional house tied well to prevent it from being blown away.

The traditional house in Jeju has no gate. Instead, they have 'Jeongnang' (gate pole). Depending on the set pattern and the number of the poles, you can tell if the owner is at home or when the owner will return. It is a unique culture that you can't find anywhere else.

It is nice to see where a village shares so much trust with its neighbours.

사진제공(김지호)-한국관광공사

I went out far away.

I will be home in the evening.

I will be home soon.

I am now at home.

넷째 주 다시 보기 DAY 16-19

Fourth week Review

이번 주 학습 내용 **Lessons This Week** -

DAY 16

◆ **A-(으)ㄴ / V-는 N** ▶ '-(으)ㄴ, -는' comes to decorate the following noun at the end of an adjective or a verb in its determiner-form.

  ⓔⅹ 우리 언니는 정말 좋은 사람이에요. My sister is a nice person.

  제가 자주 가는 곳은 커피숍이에요. I often go to a coffee shop.

◆ **안 V/A** ▶ '안' is used to express negative or opposite meaning by adding it in front of a verb or an adjective.

  ⓔⅹ 민영 씨는 고기를 안 먹어요. Minyoung doesn't eat meat.

  윤기 씨는 내일 모임에 안 올 거예요. Yoonki is not coming to the meeting tomorrow.

DAY 17

◆ **V/A-아서/어서** ▶ '-아서/어서' is applicable at the end of a verb or an adjective to explain the reason or ground.

  ⓔⅹ 그 영화가 재미있어서 두 번 봤어요. I watched the movie twice because it was funny.

  저는 커피를 좋아해서 많이 마셔요. I drink a lot of coffee because I like it.

◆ **V-고 있다** ▶ '-고 있다' is applicable at the end of a verb to describe an action continuing without an end.

  ⓔⅹ 민영 씨는 지금 케이크를 만들고 있어요. Minyoung is making a cake now.

  지금 윤기 씨가 피터 씨를 기다리고 있어요. Yoonki is waiting for Peter now.

196

파이팅!

[1-2] Listen carefully and choose the correct answer to the question.

Track 20-01

1
① 비빔밥을 좋아해요.
② 한국 노래가 좋아요.
③ 비빔밥을 안 먹어요.

2
① 지금 학교에 가고 있어요.
② 학교에 같이 가는 친구예요.
③ 머리가 너무 아파서 집에서 쉬었어요.

[3-4] Listen carefully and choose the same thing as in the conversation.

Track 20-02

3
① 남자의 친구는 경복궁에 갔어요.
② 남자는 한국 전통 문화에 관심이 많아요.
③ 남자는 여자하고 같이 안동에 갈 거예요.
④ 남자는 외국 친구하고 이야기하고 있어요.

4
① 남자는 지금 밥을 먹고 있어요.
② 여자는 영화를 보고 밥을 먹었어요.
③ 여자는 친구들하고 영화를 볼 거예요.
④ 남자는 커피숍에서 커피를 마시고 있어요.

*단어 Vocabulary

경복궁 Gyeongbokgung Palace   전통 문화 traditional culture   관심 interest
안동 Andong   외국 foreign   다른 other
하회마을 Hahoe Village   찜닭 steamed chicken

◆ **Casual speech** ▶ It is used for an informal and light tone when the speaker and listener have close relationship.

> ㉕ 가 어제 뭐 했어? What did you do yesterday?
>
> 나 친구를 만났어. I met my friend.
>
> 가 주말에 뭐 할 거야? What are you going to do on the weekend?
>
> 나 집에서 쉴 거야. I will take a rest at home.

◆ **V/A-(으)면** ▶ '-(으)면' comes at the end of a verb or an adjective assuming the situation or indicating that the preceding content becomes the basis or condition for the following.

> ㉕ 날씨가 좋으면 바다에 갈까요? Shall we go to the seaside if the weather is good?
>
> 한국에 오면 연락하세요. Please contact me if you are coming to Korea.

◆ **V/A-네요** ▶ '-네요' is used when the speaker is talking about a new fact he/she has learned through directly experiencing it, or something that is now known.

> ㉕ 오늘 날씨가 정말 춥네요. The weather is cold today.
>
> 안나 씨는 한국말을 잘하네요. Anna speaks Korean well.

◆ **못 V** ▶ '못' comes in front of a verb to say that the verb cannot perform its action.

> ㉕ 저는 춤을 못 춰요. I cannot dance.
>
> 일이 많아서 집에 일찍 못 가요. I cannot go home early because I have a lot of work.

파이팅!

Track 20-03

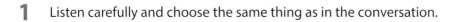

실력 다지기 Practice2

1 Listen carefully and choose the same thing as in the conversation.

① 여자는 제주도에 안 갈 거예요.

② 남자는 제주도에서 여행할 거예요.

③ 여자는 저녁에 삼겹살을 먹을 거예요.

④ 남자는 제주도에서 삼겹살을 먹었어요.

[2-3] Read the following and answer the question.

> 이제 저는 다시 고향으로 가요. 한국에서 좋은 추억을 많이 만들었어요. 그리고 좋은 사람도 많이 만났어요. 제주도가 좋아서 꼭 다시 (㉠   ). 제주도는 정말 아름다워요. 그리고 사투리도 재미있어요. 이제 공항으로 갈 거예요. 5시 비행기를 탈 거예요. 나중에 다시 꼭 올 거예요. 잘 있어요, 한국!

2 Choose the proper word for ㉠.

① 올까요　　　　　　　　　② 오세요

③ 오고 싶어요　　　　　　　④ 오고 있어요

3 Choose the same thing as in the writing.

① 이 사람은 공항에서 일해요.

② 이 사람은 제주도를 좋아해요.

③ 이 사람은 한국에 다시 왔어요.

④ 이 사람은 제주도 사투리를 잘해요.

*단어 Vocabulary

다음 달 next month	한라산 Hallasan Mountain	흑돼지 black pork	다시 again
추억 memory	사투리 dialect	공항 airport	

★ 우리만 알고 있는

여행 이야기

The Travel Story that Only We Know

📷 Beautiful tourist city in Korea

Do you know what the tourist destinations are that attract foreigners well? They are Busan and Jejudo Island! Aside from the two most famous places, Mokpo with a wonderful marina cable car and Yeosu with an amazing night sea view.

The marine cable car in Mokpo is the longest and highest in Korea, and by taking it you will be able to embrace the spectacular city and sea view at a glance.

In Sinan, a place near Mokpo, there is a Purple Island. Most of the things are purple in color. If you have anything in purple like a suit, hat or even umbrella, you can enter various sites for free! And from Purple Island, you can visit all three islands nearby as they are connected by bridges.

Besides that, there is a small city in the South Sea called Tongyeong. There are nice spots to visit, such as Hallyeosudo Cable Car, Tongyeong Undersea Tunnel (the first undersea tunnel in Asia), and Napory Farm where you can walk with your barefoot in the cypress forest to enjoy the nature.

There are also a lot of artistic villages with mural paintings everywhere in Korea. Particularly in Tongyeong, you can see nice and fun mural paintings in Dongpirang Mural Village in every alley!

맛으로
만나 보는
한국
Korea through taste

Food plays an essential role in most Korean tourist destinations. Korean food such as bibimbap and bulgogi are especially famous. Let me introduce you to some specialty food you can try in Korea.

🏅 충무 김밥 Chungmu Gimbap

Gimbap is one of the food that Korean eats a lot. It is made by rolling steamed rice and various ingredients of your choice with laver (gim). It is named according to its ingredient wrapped inside, for example, kimchi gimbap, beef gimbap, etc. It has been transformed recently into a different way of preparing it. Chungmu gimbap is different from the traditional gimbap. It is served with rice wrapped in laver and ingredients are served on the side. It can be paired with some side dishes like kkakdugi (diced radish) and squid. Although you can find Chungmu gimbap in most places, the taste is incomparable to the one sold in Tongyeong!

🏅 마산 아구찜 Masan Agujjim(Steamed Anglerfish)

Do you like spicy food? Koreans believe that eating spicy food could help to relieve stress. Hence there are many spicy foods in Korea like tteokbokki or spicy squid bibimbap. Agujjim, famous in Masan, is a must-try spicy dish. It is spicy but tasty! There is a street named after the dish in Changwon, Gyeongsang-do.

이렇게 말해요! **Say like this!**

Have you enjoyed the meal? Then, you may say the following.

잘 먹었습니다.
I really enjoyed the meal.

Appendix

01. Answer

02. Basic Korean Sentence Patterns

03. Hangeul Keyboard

DAY 01

맛있는 연습 문제 Exercise　　　　24쪽

1 ① 어　② 오　③ 이

2 ① 가지　② 거미　③ 사자　④ 나무

3 ① 아이　② 오이　③ 가구　④ 다리
　　⑤ 하나　⑥ 나비　⑦ 라디오　⑧ 아버지

DAY 02

맛있는 연습 문제 Exercise　　　　30쪽

1 ① 여　② 오　③ 요　④ 유
　　⑤ 에　⑥ 얘　⑦ 예　⑧ 야
　　⑨ 가　⑩ 토　⑪ 푸　⑫ 자

2 ① 야구　② 요리　③ 세수　④ 시계
　　⑤ 커피　⑥ 케이크　⑦ 아빠　⑧ 코끼리

DAY 03

맛있는 연습 문제 Exercise　　　　40쪽

1 ① 와　② 워　③ 의　④ 왜
　　⑤ 애　⑥ 외　⑦ 곰　⑧ 밥
　　⑨ 단　⑩ 물

DAY 04

맛있는 핵심 문법 Grammar

■ 실력 다지기 Practice1　　　　45쪽

가수예요
친구예요
학생이에요

■ 실력 다지기 Practice2　　　　45쪽

① 의사예요.
② 베트남 사람이에요.
③ 저는 회사원이에요.
④ 저는 요리사예요.
⑤ 저는 중국 사람이에요.
⑥ 저는 선생님이에요.
⑦ 저는 배우예요.

■ 실력 다지기 Practice3　　　　47쪽

① 그 사람은 의사예요.
② 저 사람은 가수예요.
③ 이 책은 제 책이에요.
④ 이 볼펜은 윤기 씨 볼펜이에요.

■ 실력 다지기 Practice4　　　　47쪽

① 저거는 또안 씨 책이에요.
② 이거는 볼펜이에요.
③ 그거는 바나나예요.

맛있는 대화 Dialog　　　　48쪽

① 또안 씨는 피터 씨의 친구예요.
② 또안 씨는 베트남 사람이에요.

맛있는 연습 문제 Exercise　　　50쪽

1 ① 일본　　② 독일　　③ 친구

2 ① 그 볼펜　　② 이 볼펜　　③ 저 볼펜

3 ① 베트남 사람이에요　　② 제 친구는
　　③ 이 책은　　④ 그거는

🎧 Listening test script

① 저는 베트남 사람이에요.
② 제 친구는 가수예요.
③ 이 책은 민영 씨 책이에요.
④ 그거는 제 볼펜이에요.

① I'm Vietnamese.
② My friend is a singer.
③ This book is Minyoung's book.
④ That is my ballpoint pen.

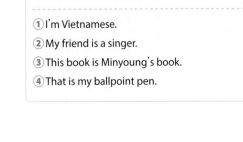

DAY 05　첫째 주 다시 보기 First week Review

◄ 실력 다지기 Practice1 ►　　53쪽

1 ① 버스　② 카드　③ 치마　④ 토마토
　　⑤ 휴지　⑥ 지우개　⑦ 얘기　⑧ 딸기
　　⑨ 남자　⑩ 운동장

◄ 실력 다지기 Practice2 ►　　55쪽

1 ① 저는 안나예요.
　　② 이 사람은 피터 씨예요.
　　③ 그 친구는 태국 사람이에요.
　　④ 저 책은 안나 씨 책이에요.

2 ① 다　　　　② 다

🎧 Listening test script

① 안녕히 계세요.
② 피터 씨는 어느 나라 사람이에요?

① Good-bye.
② What country is Peter from?

3 ① 가　　　　② 나

4 ① 저는 프랑스 사람이에요.
　　② 그 사람은 중국 사람이에요.

DAY 06

지난 학습 다시 보기 Review　　60쪽

① ✕(저는 윤기예요.)
② ○
③ ✕(저는 학생이에요.)

맛있는 핵심 문법 Grammar

◄ 실력 다지기 Practice1 ►　　63쪽

가수입니다
친구입니다
학생입니다

사천오백 원
칠천육백 원
만 이천오백 원
오만 사천 원
십만 구천팔백 원

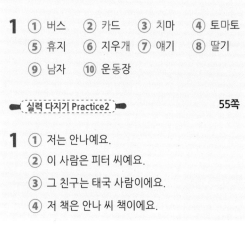

① 제 친구는 독일 사람입니다.

② 저 사람은 회사원입니다.

③ 제 동생은 대학생입니다.

④ 이윤기 씨는 한국어 선생님입니다.

만나세요
읽으세요
운동하세요
전화하세요
공부하세요

가방 한 개
물 두 병
친구 세 명

① 여기 보세요.

② 이 책 사세요.

③ 이거 두 개 주세요.

④ 잠깐만 기다리세요.

맛있는 대화 Dialog 　66쪽

① 여기는 카페예요.

② 커피는 오천 원이에요.

맛있는 연습 문제 Exercise 　68쪽

1 ① 오만 원

② 천이백 원

③ 만 육천 원

④ 이만 삼천 원(이에요/입니다)

2 ① 커피 주세요

② 얼마예요

③ 삼만 원

④ 기다리세요

🎧 **Listening test script**

① 커피 주세요.

② 얼마예요?

③ 삼만 원입니다.

④ 잠깐만 기다리세요.

- - - - - - - - - - - - - - - - - - -

① Coffee, please.

② How much is it?

③ Thirty thousand won.

④ Wait a minute.

DAY 07

지난 학습 다시 보기 Review 　70쪽

① ○

② ×(물 두 병 주세요.)

③ ×(커피 세 잔 주세요.)

맛있는 핵심 문법 Grammar

① 콜라가 있어요. 콜라가 없어요.

② 형이 있어요. 형이 없어요.

③ 카드가 있어요. 카드가 없어요.

④ 휴지가 있어요. 휴지가 없어요.

① 한국 친구가 세 명 있어요.

② 콜라가 네 병 있어요.

③ 지우개가 한 개 있어요.

④ 오빠가 두 명 있어요.

◖ 실력 다지기 Practice3 ◗　　75쪽

마셔요

책 읽어요

일어나요

세수해요

운동해요

◖ 실력 다지기 Practice4 ◗　　75쪽

① 방에서 숙제해요.

② 회사에서 일해요.

③ 지금 집에서 밥 먹어요.

④ 저는 지금 공원에서 친구 만나요.

맛있는 대화 Dialog　　76쪽

① 피터 씨는 교통 카드가 있어요.

② 교통 카드는 편의점에 있어요.

맛있는 연습 문제 Exercise　　78쪽

1 ① 있어요　② 없어요　③ 지우개가

　　④ 볼펜이　⑤ 우산이　⑥ 없어요

2 ① 휴지가　　　　② 집에서

　　③ 청소해요　　　④ 어디에서

> 🎧 Listening test script
>
> ① 교실에 휴지가 있어요.
>
> ② 지금 집에서 밥 먹어요.
>
> ③ 매일 청소해요.
>
> ④ 어디에서 사요?
>
> - - - - - - - - - - - - - - - - - - -
>
> ① There are toilet papers in the classroom.
>
> ② I'm eating at home now.
>
> ③ I clean it every day.
>
> ④ Where do you buy it?

지난 학습 다시 보기 Review　　80쪽

① ○

② ✕(도서관에서 공부해요.)

③ ○

맛있는 핵심 문법 Grammar

◖ 실력 다지기 Practice1 ◗　　83쪽

① 에　　　② 에　　　③ 에서

④ 에서　　⑤ 에

◖ 실력 다지기 Practice2 ◗　　83쪽

① 학교에

② 토요일에

③ 중국에 가요

④ 공원에 가요

> 🎧 Listening test script
>
> ① 월요일에 학교에 가요.
>
> ② 토요일에 파티가 있어요.
>
> ③ 9월 23일에 중국에 가요.
>
> ④ 주말에 공원에 가요.
>
> - - - - - - - - - - - - - - - - - - -
>
> ① I go to school on Monday.
>
> ② There is a party on Saturday.
>
> ③ I am going to China on September 23rd.
>
> ④ I go to the park on the weekend.

◖ 실력 다지기 Practice3 ◗　　85쪽

① 시험을 봐요.

② 오늘 컴퓨터를 배워요.

③ 오늘 책을 읽어요.

① 저 책도
② 바나나도
③ 콜라도

맛있는 대화 Dialog   86쪽

① 또안은 요즘도 한국어를 공부해요.
② 민영은 시험이 있어요.

맛있는 연습 문제 Exercise   88쪽

1   ① 공원에   ② 교실에
    ③ 한국어를   ④ 일본 사람도

> 🎧 **Listening test script**
>
> ① 내일 공원에 가요.
> ② 교실에 시계가 있어요.
> ③ 매일 도서관에서 한국어를 공부해요.
> ④ 우리 반에 중국 사람이 있어요. 일본 사람도
>   있어요.
>
> ---
>
> ① I'm going to the park tomorrow.
> ② There is a clock in the classroom.
> ③ I study Korean at the library every day.
> ④ There is a Chinese in my class. There are also
>   Japanese.

2   ① 시장에 가요
    ② 저도 치킨을 좋아해요
    ③ 또안 씨도 파티에 가요
    ④ 학교 앞에서 만나요

DAY 09

지난 학습 다시 보기 Review   90쪽

① ○
② ✕(피터 씨는 친구를 만나요.)
③ ✕(민영 씨는 학교에서 공부해요.)

맛있는 핵심 문법 Grammar

비싸요
맛있어요
맛없어요
재미없어요
따뜻해요
시원해요

① 친구가 많아요.
② 날씨가 맑아요.
③ 한국어 공부가 재미있어요.
④ 비빔밥이 좋아요.

바빠요
배가 고파요
날씨가 나빠요
편지를 써요
불을 꺼요

① 머리가 아파요.
② 가방이 예뻐요.
③ 기분이 나빠요.
④ 모자를 써요.

맛있는 대화 Dialog   96쪽

① 여기는 한복 가게예요.

② 한복이 예뻐요.

맛있는 연습 문제 Exercise   98쪽

1
- ① 예뻐요
- ② 비싸요
- ③ 따뜻해요
- ④ 아파요

> 🎧 Listening test script
>
> ① 한복이 예뻐요.
>
> ② 시계가 비싸요.
>
> ③ 날씨가 따뜻해요.
>
> ④ 다리가 아파요.
>
> ---
>
> ① The hanbok is pretty.
>
> ② Watches are expensive.
>
> ③ The weather is warm.
>
> ④ My leg hurts.

2
- ① 나빠요
- ② 맛있어요
- ③ 재미있어요
- ④ 아파요

둘째 주 다시 보기 Second week Review

🔈 실력 다지기 Practice1   101쪽

1
- ① 제 친구는 한국 사람입니다.
- ② 커피 한 잔 주세요.
- ③ 지금 노트북이 없어요.
- ④ 저는 노래방에서 노래해요.

2 ③   **3** ②   **4** ①

> 🎧 Listening test script
>
> **2** 이 가방 얼마예요?
>
> **3** 한국어 책이 있어요?
>
> **4** 지금 뭐 해요?
>
> ---
>
> **2** How much is this bag?
>
> **3** Do you have any Korean book?
>
> **4** What are you doing now?

5 ① 가   ② 나

> 🎧 Listening test script
>
> ① 남 여기요. 비빔밥 하나 주세요.
>
>   여 네. 잠깐만 기다리세요.
>
> ② 남 이 신발 얼마예요?
>
>   여 오만 원입니다.
>
> ---
>
> ① M Here. One bibimbap, please.
>
>   W Yes, wait a minute.
>
> ② M How much are these shoes?
>
>   W It's fifty thousand won.

🔈 실력 다지기 Practice2   103쪽

1
- ① 윤기 씨는 공원에 가요.
- ② 안나 씨는 태권도를 배워요.
- ③ 또안 씨는 오늘 바빠요.
- ④ 제 고양이가 예뻐요.

2 ②   **3** ①   **4** ②

> 🎧 Listening test script
>
> **2** 책이 어디에 있어요?
>
> **3** 가방이 예뻐요.
>
> **4** 이 영화가 재미있어요?
>
> ---
>
> **2** Where are the books?
>
> **3** The bag is beautiful.
>
> **4** Is this movie interesting?

5 ①

DAY 11

지난 학습 다시 보기 Review   108쪽

① ✕(가방이 비싸요.)

② ✕(윤기 씨는 요즘 바빠요.)

③ ✕(날씨가 따뜻해요.)

맛있는 핵심 문법 Grammar

▬〔 실력 다지기 Practice1 〕▬   111쪽

친구를 만날 거예요

한국어를 공부할 거예요

밥을 먹을 거예요

옷을 입을 거예요

▬〔 실력 다지기 Practice2 〕▬   111쪽

① 쇼핑할 거예요

② 쉴 거예요

③ 읽을 거예요

④ 여행할 거예요

▬〔 실력 다지기 Practice3 〕▬   113쪽

책하고 볼펜

휴대 전화하고 교통 카드

밥하고 라면

▬〔 실력 다지기 Practice4 〕▬   113쪽

① 민영 씨하고 같이 도서관에 가요

② 콜라하고 우유를 사요

③ 동생하고 백화점에서 쇼핑할 거예요

④ 사과하고 피자를 좋아해요

맛있는 대화 Dialog   114쪽

① 또안 씨는 주말에 파티를 할 거예요.

② 파티는 또안 씨 집에서 할 거예요.

맛있는 연습 문제 Exercise   116쪽

1 ① 책을 읽을 거예요

② 영화를 볼 거예요

③ 청소할 거예요

④ 운동할 거예요

2 ① 학교에 갈 거예요

② 빵하고 우유를

③ 친구하고 / 갈 거예요

DAY 12

지난 학습 다시 보기 Review 118쪽

① ◯
② ◯
③ ✕(형하고 영화를 볼 거예요.)

맛있는 핵심 문법 Grammar

◀ 실력 다지기 Practice1 ▶ 121쪽

왔어요
읽었어요
만났어요
기다렸어요
운동했어요

비쌌어요
맛있었어요
재미없었어요
따뜻했어요
시원했어요

◀ 실력 다지기 Practice2 ▶ 121쪽

① 주말에 백화점에 갔어요.
② 그 영화가 재미있었어요.
③ 어제 좀 피곤했어요.
④ 어제 집에서 청소했어요.
⑤ 친구하고 카페에서 숙제했어요.

◀ 실력 다지기 Practice3 ▶ 123쪽

밥을 먹고 싶어요
책을 읽고 싶어요
영화를 보고 싶어요
공원에서 산책하고 싶어요
집에서 운동하고 싶어요

◀ 실력 다지기 Practice4 ▶ 123쪽

① 콘서트에 가고 싶어요.
② 청바지를 사고 싶어요.
③ 그 노래를 듣고 싶어요.
④ 그 배우를 만나고 싶어요.
⑤ 케이크를 만들고 싶어요.

맛있는 대화 Dialog 124쪽

① 안나 씨는 지난 주말에 머드 축제에 갔어요.
② 안나 씨하고 민영 씨는 다음 주말에 동강에 갈 거예요.

맛있는 연습 문제 Exercise 126쪽

1 ① 재미있었어요
② 쉬었어요
③ 만났어요

2 ① 타고 싶어요
② 가고 싶어요
③ 사고 싶어요

DAY 13

지난 학습 다시 보기 Review 128쪽

① ◯
② ✕(커피를 마시고 싶어요.)
③ ✕(어제 한국어를 공부했어요.)

맛있는 핵심 문법 Grammar

━●━ 실력 다지기 Practice1 ━●━   131쪽

① 로   ② 로

③ 로   ④ 으로

━●━ 실력 다지기 Practice2 ━●━   131쪽

① 배로   ② 휴대 전화로

③ 한국말로   ④ 택시로

━●━ 실력 다지기 Practice3 ━●━   133쪽

① 떡볶이가 매워요.

② 시험이 쉬워요.

③ 인형이 귀여워요.

④ 경치가 아름다워요.

━●━ 실력 다지기 Practice4 ━●━   133쪽

① 날씨가 추웠어요.

② 음식이 매웠어요.

③ 제 동생이 귀여웠어요.

④ 가방이 가벼웠어요.

맛있는 대화 Dialog   134쪽

① 서울에서 경주까지 KTX로 두 시간쯤 걸려요.

② 경주는 정말 아름다워요.

맛있는 연습 문제 Exercise   136쪽

1   ① 아름다워요

     ② 지하철로 가세요

     ③ 더워요

     ④ 기차로 갈 거예요

🎧 **Listening test script**

① 한국은 정말 아름다워요.

② 명동까지 지하철로 가세요.

③ 오늘 날씨가 정말 더워요.

④ 서울에서 부산까지 기차로 갈 거예요.

- -

① Korea is really beautiful.

② Take the subway to Myeong-dong.

③ The weather is really hot today.

④ I will go from Seoul to Busan by train.

2   ① 추워요

     ② 귀여워요

     ③ 지하철로 가요

     ④ 버스로 한 시간쯤 걸려요

DAY 14

지난 학습 다시 보기 Review   138쪽

① ✕ (시험이 쉬워요.)

② ✕ (명동까지 지하철로 가세요.)

③ ○

맛있는 핵심 문법 Grammar

━●━ 실력 다지기 Practice1 ━●━   141쪽

밥을 먹을까요?

책을 읽을까요?

주말에 만날까요?

공원에서 산책할까요?

도서관에서 공부할까요?

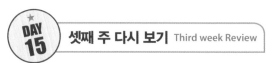

◀═ 실력 다지기 Practice2 ═▶   141쪽

① 같이 축구를 할까요?

② 같이 커피를 마실까요?

③ 백화점 앞에서 만날까요?

④ 같이 학교에 갈까요?

◀═ 실력 다지기 Practice3 ═▶   143쪽

① 청소하고 쉬었어요.

② 책을 읽고 커피를 마셨어요.

③ 학교에서 공부하고 운동했어요.

④ 수업이 끝나고 노래방에 갔어요.

◀═ 실력 다지기 Practice4 ═▶   143쪽

① 음식이 싸고 맛있어요.

② 동생이 귀엽고 예뻐요.

③ 주말에 밥을 먹고 빵도 먹어요.

맛있는 대화 Dialog   144쪽

① 두 사람은 지금 커피를 마시고 있어요.

② 피터 씨는 다음 주에 전주로 출장을 가요.

맛있는 연습 문제 Exercise   146쪽

1 ① 칠까요   ② 만날까요
　 ③ 볼까요   ④ 공부할까요

2 ① 밥을 먹고   ② 운동하고
　 ③ 시험이 끝나고   ④ 친구를 만나고

> 🎧 Listening test script
>
> ① 밥을 먹고 숙제해요.
>
> ② 운동하고 샤워할 거예요.
>
> ③ 시험이 끝나고 여행 갈 거예요.
>
> ④ 친구를 만나고 집에 갔어요.

> ① I eat and do my homework.
>
> ② I will exercise and take a shower.
>
> ③ After the exam, I will go on a trip.
>
> ④ I met a friend and went home.

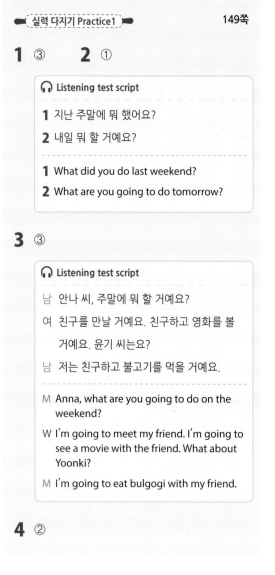

DAY 15 셋째 주 다시 보기 Third week Review

◀═ 실력 다지기 Practice1 ═▶   149쪽

1 ③   **2** ①

> 🎧 Listening test script
>
> **1** 지난 주말에 뭐 했어요?
>
> **2** 내일 뭐 할 거예요?
>
> - - - - - - - - - - - - - - -
>
> **1** What did you do last weekend?
>
> **2** What are you going to do tomorrow?

3 ③

> 🎧 Listening test script
>
> 남 안나 씨, 주말에 뭐 할 거예요?
>
> 여 친구를 만날 거예요. 친구하고 영화를 볼 거예요. 윤기 씨는요?
>
> 남 저는 친구하고 불고기를 먹을 거예요.
>
> - - - - - - - - - - - - - - -
>
> M Anna, what are you going to do on the weekend?
>
> W I'm going to meet my friend. I'm going to see a movie with the friend. What about Yoonki?
>
> M I'm going to eat bulgogi with my friend.

4 ②

◀▬ 실력 다지기 Practice2 ▬▶   151쪽

1 ③

> 🎧 Listening test script
>
> 남 토요일에 뭐 해요?
>
> 여 별일 없어요. 왜요?
>
> 남 토요일에 케이팝 콘서트가 있어요. 같이 가요.
>
> 여 케이팝 콘서트요? 좋아요. 어디에서 해요?
>
> 남 잠실에서 7시에 해요.
>
> 여 네. 그럼 우리 잠실역에서 만날까요?
>
> 남 네. 좋아요.
>
> ---
>
> M What are you doing on Saturday?
>
> W It's nothing special. Why?
>
> M There is a K-pop concert on Saturday. Let's go together.
>
> W A K-pop concert? I like it. Where do they do it?
>
> M They do it at 7 o'clock in Jamsil.
>
> W Yes. Then shall we meet at Jamsil Station?
>
> M Yes, that's fine.

2 ②   **3** ③

DAY 16

지난 학습 다시 보기 Review   156쪽

① ○

② ✕(커피숍에서 공부할까요?)

③ ○

맛있는 핵심 문법 Grammar

◀▬ 실력 다지기 Practice1 ▬▶   159쪽

좋아하는 책

바쁜 친구

맛있는 음식

무거운 가방

◀▬ 실력 다지기 Practice2 ▬▶   159쪽

① 마시는

② 슬픈

③ 좋은

④ 듣는

◀▬ 실력 다지기 Practice3 ▬▶   161쪽

집에 안 와요

술을 안 마셔요

책을 안 읽어요

청소 안 해요

안 비싸요

안 따뜻해요

◀▬ 실력 다지기 Practice4 ▬▶   161쪽

① 길이 안 막혔어요.

② 마음에 안 들었어요.

③ 케이크를 안 만들었어요.

④ 시험이 안 끝났어요.

맛있는 대화 Dialog   162쪽

① 대구는 윤기 씨가 좋아하는 곳이에요.

② 또안 씨는 밥을 안 먹었어요.

맛있는 연습 문제 Exercise   164쪽

1   ① 맛있는 케이크를   ② 무서운 영화를

      ③ 만나는 사람이   ④ 사랑하는 사람이에요

① 제가 맛있는 케이크를 만들었어요.

② 저는 무서운 영화를 싫어해요.

③ 요즘 만나는 사람이 있어요?

④ 윤기 씨는 제가 정말 사랑하는 사람이에요.

---

① I made a delicious cake.

② I hate scary movies.

③ Is there anyone you meet these days?

④ Yoonki is the person I really love.

2
① 안 마셔요
② 안 만났어요
③ 안 갈 거예요
④ 노래 안 해요

DAY 17

지난 학습 다시 보기 Review 166쪽

① ○

② ✕(저 영화는 정말 무서운 영화예요.)

③ ✕(형은 공부 안 해요.)

맛있는 핵심 문법 Grammar

실력 다지기 Practice1 169쪽

① 사과가 싸서 많이 샀어요.

② 날씨가 추워서 집에 있었어요.

③ 커피를 많이 마셔서 잠이 안 왔어요.

실력 다지기 Practice2 169쪽

① 길이 막혀서

② 너무 재미있어서

③ 도와줘서

실력 다지기 Practice3 171쪽

책을 읽고 있어요

집에서 쉬고 있어요

공원에서 산책하고 있어요

도서관에서 공부하고 있어요

실력 다지기 Practice4 171쪽

① 보고 있어요

② 구경하고 있어요

③ 찾고 있어요

④ 가고 있어요

맛있는 대화 Dialog 172쪽

① 민영 씨는 안나 씨하고 울산에 왔어요.

② 민영 씨는 지금 여기저기 구경하고 있어요.

맛있는 연습 문제 Exercise 174쪽

1
① 아파서
② 있어서
③ 자서
④ 와서

2
① 읽고 있어요
② 배우고 있어요
③ 청소하고 있어요

① 동생은 지금 책을 읽고 있어요.

② 요즘 한국어를 배우고 있어요.

③ 형은 지금 청소하고 있어요.

---

① My younger brother is reading a book now.

② I am learning Korean these days.

③ My elder brother is cleaning right now.

지난 학습 다시 보기 Review　176쪽

① ○

② ×(같이 가고 싶어서 갔어요.)

③ ○

맛있는 핵심 문법 Grammar

실력 다지기 Practice1　179쪽

집에 왔어.

커피를 마실 거야.

책을 읽을까?

청소하고 있어.

비싸.

따뜻해.

내 휴대 전화야.

실력 다지기 Practice2　179쪽

① 가방이 무거워.

② 테니스를 쳐.

③ 공원에서 산책해.

④ 한국 노래를 좋아해.

실력 다지기 Practice3　181쪽

① 날씨가 좋으면 공원에 갈 거예요.

② 시험이 끝나면 부산에서 여행할 거예요.

③ 한국에 가면 이태원에서 밥을 먹을 거예요.

실력 다지기 Practice4　181쪽

① 늦으면

② 괜찮으면

③ 출발하면

맛있는 대화 Dialog　182쪽

① 또안과 민영은 말을 놓았어요.

② 두 사람은 안나를 기다리고 있어요.

맛있는 연습 문제 Exercise　184쪽

1
① 처음이야　② 곳이야
③ 맞아　④ 내가
⑤ 곳이야　⑥ 안 먹었어
⑦ 먹을까　⑧ 응

2
① 날씨가 좋으면
② 아프면
③ 방학이 되면
④ 아이스크림을 많이 먹으면

> 🎧 Listening test script
>
> ① 날씨가 좋으면 산책할 거예요.
> ② 아프면 집에서 쉬세요.
> ③ 방학이 되면 여행을 할 거예요.
> ④ 아이스크림을 많이 먹으면 배가 아파요.
>
> -
>
> ① If the weather is nice, I will go for a walk.
> ② If you are sick, rest at home.
> ③ I'm going to travel when I'm on school vacation.
> ④ If I eat a lot of ice cream, my stomach hurts.

지난 학습 다시 보기 Review　186쪽

① ○

② ×(지금 공부해.)

③ ×(배고프면 밥 먹자.)

맛있는 핵심 문법 Grammar

실력 다지기 Practice1   189쪽

운동을 잘하네요
눈이 많이 오네요
날씨가 맑네요
시험이 어렵네요
동생이 예쁘네요

실력 다지기 Practice2   189쪽

① 아름답네요
② 읽네요
③ 왔네요
④ 했네요

실력 다지기 Practice3   191쪽

영화를 못 봐요
술을 못 마셔요
친구를 못 만나요
운동 못 해요
청소 못 해요

실력 다지기 Practice4   191쪽

① 못 갔어요
② 못 사요
③ 못 했어요
④ 못 타요

맛있는 대화 Dialog   192쪽

① 두 사람이 지금 있는 곳은 드라마에도 많이 나왔어요.
② 안나 씨는 지난번에 비가 많이 와서 우도에 못 갔어요.

맛있는 연습 문제 Exercise   194쪽

1
① 고프네요
② 심심하네요
③ 공부하네요

2
① 못 해요
② 못 먹어요
③ 못 자서
④ 못 해서

🎧 **Listening test script**

① 저는 운동을 못 해요.
② 제 친구는 고기를 못 먹어요.
③ 잠을 못 자서 너무 피곤해요.
④ 수영을 못 해서 수영장에 안 가요.

① I can't exercise.
② My friend can't eat meat.
③ I'm so tired because I couldn't sleep.
④ I can't swim, so I don't go to the pool.

DAY 20 넷째 주 다시 보기 Fourth week Review

실력 다지기 Practice1   197쪽

1 ①   **2** ③

🎧 **Listening test script**

1 좋아하는 음식이 뭐예요?
2 어제 왜 학교에 안 왔어요?

1 What is your favorite food?
2 Why didn't you come to school yesterday?

3 ①　　**4** ③

Listening test script

3 남　제 친구가 한국에 와요. 그 친구하고 어
　　　디에 가면 좋을까요? 제 친구는 한국 전
　　　통 문화에 관심이 많아요.

　　여　경복궁에는 갔어요?

　　남　네. 그 친구랑 서울에 많이 가서 이번에
　　　는 다른 곳에 가고 싶어요.

　　여　그럼 안동은요? 안동은 하회마을도 유
　　　명하고 찜닭도 맛있어요.

　　남　아, 안동은 안 갔어요. 고마워요.

4 여　여보세요. 윤기 씨, 지금 뭐 해요?

　　남　집에서 쉬고 있어요.

　　여　안나 씨하고 피터 씨하고 같이 영화를
　　　볼 거예요. 윤기 씨도 같이 가요.

　　남　네. 좋아요.

　　여　우리가 자주 가는 커피숍으로 오세요.
　　　그런데 밥 먹었어요?

　　남　아니요. 안 먹었어요.

　　여　우리도 안 먹었어요. 밥 먼저 먹고 영화
　　　를 볼까요?

　　남　네. 좋아요.

3 M　My friend is coming to Korea. Which
　　　places will be good for us two to visit
　　　together? My friend is very interested
　　　in Korean traditional culture.

　　W　Did you go to Gyeongbokgung
　　　Palace?

　　M　Yes. I went to Seoul a lot with that
　　　friend, and this time I want to go
　　　somewhere else.

　　W　Then what about Andong? Andong
　　　is famous for Hahoe Village, and the
　　　steamed chicken is delicious.

　　M　Oh, I didn't go to Andong. Thank you.

4 W　Hello. Yoonki, what are you doing
　　　now?

　　M　I'm resting at home.

　　W　Anna and Peter are going to watch a
　　　movie together. Yoonki, will you also
　　　go?

　　M　Yes. I like it.

　　W　Come to the coffee shop we frequent.
　　　But, did you have a meal?

　　M　No. I didn't have, yet.

　　W　We didn't have either. Shall we have
　　　meals first and then watch a movie?

　　M　Yes. That's fine.

◀══ 실력 다지기 Practice2 ══▶　　199쪽

1 ②

Listening test script

　　남　다음 달에 제주도에 갈 거야.

　　여　정말? 제주도에 가면 한라산에 꼭 가. 경치
　　　도 아름답고 좋아.

　　남　또 제주도에서 뭘 먹으면 좋을까?

　　여　고기를 좋아하면 흑돼지 삼겹살을 꼭 먹어.
　　　정말 맛있어.

　　M　I'm going to Jejudo Island next month.

　　W　Really? If you go to Jejudo Island, be sure
　　　to visit Hallasan Mountain. The scenery is
　　　also beautiful and nice.

　　M　What else should I eat on Jejudo Island?

　　W　If you like meat, you must try the black
　　　pork samgyeopsal. Really delicious.

2 ③　　**3** ②

Basic Korean Sentence Patterns

▶ **Adjective**

	A-아요/어요 be A	A-았어요/었어요 was A	A-는 N A+N	안 A not A
	p.92	p.120	p.158	p.160
싸다 cheap	싸요	쌌어요	싼 옷	안 싸요
좋다 good	좋아요	좋았어요	좋은 사람	안 좋아요
비싸다 expensive	비싸요	비쌌어요	비싼 가방	안 비싸요
맛있다 delicious	맛있어요	맛있었어요	맛있는 떡볶이	안 맛있어요
맛없다 tasteless	맛없어요	맛없었어요	맛없는 빵	안 맛없어요
재미있다 fun	재미있어요	재미있었어요	재미있는 영화	안 재미있어요
재미없다 boring	재미없어요	재미없었어요	재미없는 파티	안 재미없어요
깨끗하다 clean	깨끗해요	깨끗했어요	깨끗한 교실	안 깨끗해요
따뜻하다 warm	따뜻해요	따뜻했어요	따뜻한 집	안 따뜻해요
시원하다 cool	시원해요	시원했어요	시원한 물	안 시원해요
피곤하다 tired	피곤해요	피곤했어요	피곤한 월요일	안 피곤해요
춥다 cold	추워요	추웠어요	추운 날씨	안 추워요
맵다 spicy	매워요	매웠어요	매운 음식	안 매워요
어렵다 difficult	어려워요	어려웠어요	어려운 일	안 어려워요
예쁘다 pretty	예뻐요	예뻤어요	예쁜 구두	안 예뻐요
바쁘다 busy	바빠요	바빴어요	바쁜 친구	안 바빠요

p.168	p.178	p.178	p.180	p.188
A-아서/어서 because A	**A-아/어** be A	**A-았어/었어** was A	**A-(으)면** if A	**A-네요** be A
싸서	싸	쌌어	싸면	싸네요
좋아서	좋아	좋았어	좋으면	좋네요
비싸서	비싸	비쌌어	비싸면	비싸네요
맛있어서	맛있어	맛있었어	맛있으면	맛있네요
맛없어서	맛없어	맛없었어	맛없으면	맛없네요
재미있어서	재미있어	재미있었어	재미있으면	재미있네요
재미없어서	재미없어	재미없었어	재미없으면	재미없네요
깨끗해서	깨끗해	깨끗했어	깨끗하면	깨끗하네요
따뜻해서	따뜻해	따뜻했어	따뜻하면	따뜻하네요
시원해서	시원해	시원했어	시원하면	시원하네요
피곤해서	피곤해	피곤했어	피곤하면	피곤하네요
추워서	추워	추웠어	추우면	춥네요
매워서	매워	매웠어	매우면	맵네요
어려워서	어려워	어려웠어	어려우면	어렵네요
예뻐서	예뻐	예뻤어	예쁘면	예쁘네요
바빠서	바빠	바빴어	바쁘면	바쁘네요

▶ Verb

	V-(으)세요 please V	V-아요/어요 V	V-(으)ㄹ 거예요 will V	V-았어요/었어요 V+-ed
	p.64	p.74	p.110	p.120
가다 go	가세요	가요	갈 거예요	갔어요
사다 buy	사세요	사요	살 거예요	샀어요
앉다 sit	앉으세요	앉아요	앉을 거예요	앉았어요
만나다 meet	만나세요	만나요	만날 거예요	만났어요
보다 see	보세요	봐요	볼 거예요	봤어요
먹다 eat	드세요	먹어요	먹을 거예요	먹었어요
읽다 read	읽으세요	읽어요	읽을 거예요	읽었어요
쉬다 take a rest	쉬세요	쉬어요	쉴 거예요	쉬었어요
마시다 drink	마시세요	마셔요	마실 거예요	마셨어요
배우다 learn	배우세요	배워요	배울 거예요	배웠어요
일하다 work	일하세요	일해요	일할 거예요	일했어요
공부하다 study	공부하세요	공부해요	공부할 거예요	공부했어요
쇼핑하다 go shopping	쇼핑하세요	쇼핑해요	쇼핑할 거예요	쇼핑했어요
전화하다 call	전화하세요	전화해요	전화할 거예요	전화했어요
듣다 listen	들으세요	들어요	들을 거예요	들었어요
쓰다 write	쓰세요	써요	쓸 거예요	썼어요

| p.122 | p.140 | p.142 | p.158 | p.160 | p.168 |

V-고 싶다 want to V	V-(으)ㄹ까요? Shall we V?	V-고 V and	V-는 N N that V	안 V not V	V-아서/어서 because V
가고 싶다	갈까요?	가고	가는 사람	안 가요	가서
사고 싶다	살까요?	사고	사는 옷	안 사요	사서
앉고 싶다	앉을까요?	앉고	앉는 의자	안 앉아요	앉아서
만나고 싶다	만날까요?	만나고	만나는 친구	안 만나요	만나서
보고 싶다	볼까요?	보고	보는 영화	안 봐요	봐서
먹고 싶다	먹을까요?	먹고	먹는 음식	안 먹어요	먹어서
읽고 싶다	읽을까요?	읽고	읽는 책	안 읽어요	읽어서
쉬고 싶다	쉴까요?	쉬고	쉬는 주말	안 쉬어요	쉬어서
마시고 싶다	마실까요?	마시고	마시는 커피	안 마셔요	마셔서
배우고 싶다	배울까요?	배우고	배우는 한국어	안 배워요	배워서
일하고 싶다	일할까요?	일하고	일하는 회사	일 안 해요	일해서
공부하고 싶다	공부할까요?	공부하고	공부하는 교실	공부 안 해요	공부해서
쇼핑하고 싶다	쇼핑할까요?	쇼핑하고	쇼핑하는 백화점	쇼핑 안 해요	쇼핑해서
전화하고 싶다	전화할까요?	전화하고	전화하는 동생	전화 안 해요	전화해서
듣고 싶다	들을까요?	듣고	듣는 노래	안 들어요	들어서
쓰고 싶다	쓸까요?	쓰고	쓰는 편지	안 써요	써서

V-고 있다 V+-ing	V-았어/었어 V+-ed	V-(으)ㄹ 거야 will V	V-(으)면 if V	V-네요 V	못 V can not V
가고 있다	갔어	갈 거야	가면	가네요	못 가요
사고 있다	샀어	살 거야	사면	사네요	못 사요
앉자 있다	앉았어	앉을 거야	앉으면	앉네요	못 앉아요
만나고 있다	만났어	만날 거야	만나면	만나네요	못 만나요
보고 있다	봤어	볼 거야	보면	보네요	못 봐요
먹고 있다	먹었어	먹을 거야	먹으면	먹네요	못 먹어요
읽고 있다	읽었어	읽을 거야	읽으면	읽네요	못 읽어요
쉬고 있다	쉬었어	쉴 거야	쉬면	쉬네요	못 쉬어요
마시고 있다	마셨어	마실 거야	마시면	마시네요	못 마셔요
배우고 있다	배웠어	배울 거야	배우면	배우네요	못 배워요
일하고 있다	일했어	일할 거야	일하면	일하네요	일 못 해요
공부하고 있다	공부했어	공부할 거야	공부하면	공부하네요	공부 못 해요
쇼핑하고 있다	쇼핑했어	쇼핑할 거야	쇼핑하면	쇼핑하네요	쇼핑 못 해요
전화하고 있다	전화했어	전화할 거야	전화하면	전화하네요	전화 못 해요
듣고 있다	들었어	들을 거야	들으면	듣네요	못 들어요
쓰고 있다	썼어	쓸 거야	쓰면	쓰네요	못 써요

Hangeul Keyboard

❶ ㅃ : shift key & ㅂ
❷ ㅉ : shift key & ㅈ
❸ ㄸ : shift key & ㄷ
❹ ㄲ : shift key & ㄱ

❺ ㅆ : shift key & ㅅ
❻ ㅐ : shift key & ㅐ
❼ ㅔ : shift key & ㅔ

맛있는 books

한글 Hangeul

자음 Consonants

ㄱ [k/g]  가구 furniture	**ㄴ** [n]  나무 tree	**ㄷ** [t/d]  다리 leg	**ㄹ** [r/l]  다리미 iron
ㅁ [m]  어머니 mother	**ㅂ** [p/b]  바다 sea	**ㅅ** [s]  사자 lion	**ㅇ** [ø]  아이 child
ㅈ [ʧ/j]  지우개 eraser	**ㅊ** [ʧʰ]  치마 skirt	**ㅋ** [kʰ] 커피 coffee	**ㅌ** [tʰ]  기타 guitar
ㅍ [pʰ]  피자 pizza	**ㅎ** [h]  하마 hippo	**ㄲ** [k'] 토끼 rabbit	**ㄸ** [t']  따뜻하다 warm
ㅃ [p']  오빠 elder/older brother	**ㅆ** [s']  아저씨 middle-aged man	**ㅉ** [ʧ']  짜다 salty	

모음 Vowels

ㅏ [a]

사
four

ㅑ [ya]

야구
baseball

ㅓ [ə]

거미
spider

ㅕ [yə]

여자
woman

ㅗ [o]

오이
cucumber

ㅛ [yo]

요리
cooking

ㅜ [u]

구두
shoes

ㅠ [yu]

우유
milk

ㅡ [ɨ]
카드
card

ㅣ [i]
바지
pants

ㅐ [ɛ]

배
ship

ㅒ [yɛ]

얘기
story

ㅔ [e]
게
crab

ㅖ [ye]

시계
clock, watch

ㅘ [wa]

사과
apple

ㅝ [wə]

뭐
what

ㅟ [wi]
귀
ear

ㅢ [ɰi]
의사
doctor

ㅚ [we]
회사
company

ㅙ [wɛ]

돼지
pig

ㅞ [we]
스웨터
sweater